Of Orphans
and Warriors

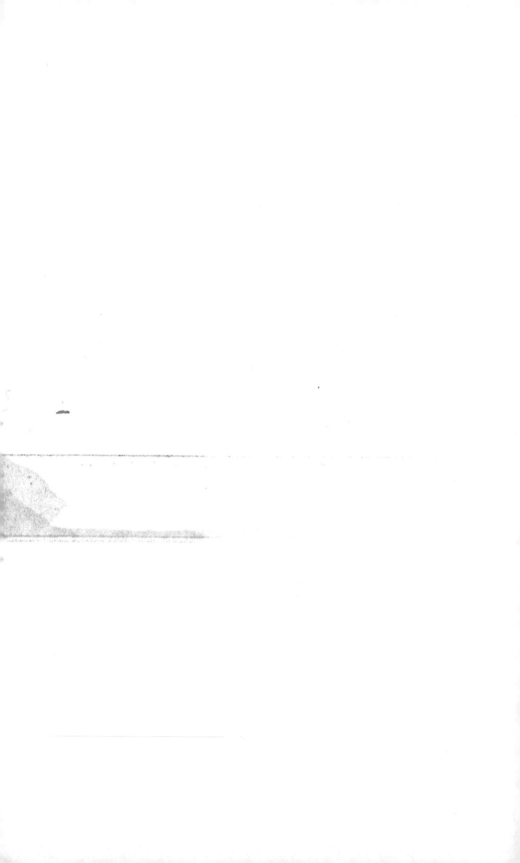

Of Orphans and Warriors

Inventing Chinese American Culture and Identity

Gloria Heyung Chun

Rutgers University Press

New Brunswick, New Jersey, and London

Library of Congress Cataloging-in-Publication Data

Chun, Gloria H., 1961–
    Of orphans and warriors : inventing Chinese American culture and
identity / Gloria H. Chun.
      p. cm.
    Includes bibliographical references (p.) and index.
    ISBN 0–8135–2708–2 (alk. paper). — ISBN 0–8135–2709–0 (pbk. :
alk. paper)
    1. Chinese Americans—History. 2. Chinese Americans—Ethnic
identity. 3. Chinese Americans—Cultural assimilation. 4. Chinese
Americans—California—History. 5. Chinese Americans—California—
Ethnic identity. 6. Chinese Americans—California—Cultural
assimilation. I. Title
E184.C5C56   2000
305.895'1073'0904—dc21   99–33564
                                                  CIP

British Cataloging-in-Publication data for this book is available from the British
Library

Manufactured in the United States of America

For lifelong guidance
I thank my parents, Miriam and Paul Chun,
For his big heart and encouragement,
Thomas Dandelet, my love,
For laughter and perspective
My daughter, Sophia

Contents

Acknowledgments

This project was the work of many hands. I am immeasurably indebted to my colleagues and professors at the University of California at Berkeley for seeing my project through from beginning to end. To Ronald Takaki for unwavering support and instructive criticisms and to Ling-chi Wang for sharing his expertise in the area and providing me leads, I am especially thankful. For their insights and lessons in Chinese America, I want to thank Ben Tong, Frank Chin, Judy Yung, and Him Mark Lai. Wei-chi Poon, the head librarian at the Asian American Studies Library at Berkeley, and the archival staff at The Bancroft Library, the Hoover Institute, and the Library at the Asian American Studies Center at the University of California at Los Angeles, all deserve much praise for their ability to track down resources. I also want to thank those who have read portions of my manuscript in its various stages and have made valuable comments: Kevin Scott Wong, Sucheng Chan, Sarah Willie, Amy Cheng, Sanjib Baruah, Mark Lytle, Mario Bick, Myra Armstead, and Alice Stroup. I am especially grateful to my research assistants, Katheryn Yep and Ellen Wu. I also want to recognize those who have given me their precious time to be interviewed: Laureen Chew, David Gan, Floyd Huen, Gordon Lau, Jean Quon, Paul Wing, Alfred Wong, Jade Snow Wong, and Jadin Wong. In addition I want to thank Leslie Mitchner, editor in chief, and Marilyn Campbell, managing editor, and Adaya Henis, copyeditor, at Rutgers University Press for their meticulous, careful reading, cheerfulness, and encouragement. Finally, I want to thank my students and colleagues at Bard College for their intellectual guidance and encouragement.

Of Orphans
and Warriors

I speak nothing but the mother tongue bein' born to none of my own, I talk the talk of orphans.

—Tam Lum, in Frank Chin's *Chickencoop Chinaman*

I inspired my army, and I fed them. At night I sang to them glorious songs that came out of the sky and into my head. When I opened my mouth, the songs poured out and were loud enough for the whole encampment to hear.

—the Woman Warrior, in Maxine Hong Kingston's
The Woman Warrior

Know the enemy and know yourself; in a hundred battles you will never be in peril.

—Sun Tzu, *The Art of War*

Introduction

"We were as American as can be," said Jadin Wong in recalling the days when she used to dance at a nightclub noted for its line of exotic dancers and Sinatra-esque singers. In the 1940s, a club like hers, the Forbidden City, could be found in any large city. What was unusual about this one was that it was in Chinatown, San Francisco. Jadin Wong belonged to an all-Chinese chorus line at a time when Asians were addressed as "Orientals" and when many Americans thought that Chinese women had bound feet. In light of this, what did it mean for Ms. Wong, an American-born Chinese, to say that she thought of herself as an "American"?[1]

For countless American-born Chinese like Jadin Wong, who occupied a marginal status in society, the question of identity was inescapable.[2] Identity has remained a central preoccupation for Chinese Americans, given the delegitimization of traditional terms of reference, and of their cultural difference, by mainstream America. *Of Orphans and Warriors: Inventing Chinese American Culture and Identity* provides a window onto the way in which American-born Chinese negotiated their identity over a span of several decades. The phrase "of orphans and warriors" underscores both the struggles and the opportunities unique to American-born generations. Like orphans, they came to occupy a marginalized position sandwiched between generations, cultures, languages, and geographies. Even as they resented being measured by the ethnicity standards of the immigrant generation, they also refused to succumb to American mainstreaming. And while their doubly marginalized position as second-generation Chinese Americans easily became their "riverbanks of life," as described by Maxine Hong Kingston, delimiting their opportunities to live and work in America, at other times, their liminal position as the American-born Chinese offered them unprecedented opportunities to negotiate an enabling position and identity in the wider society.[3] Serving as a bridge between the parental community and society at large, they acted as political representatives, translators, ethnographers, cultural advance guards, and entertainers staging Chinese American culture and identity for the broader public. Being so orphaned predisposed them to become warriors, poised to safeguard their parental, ethnic community as well as to carve out new opportunities for themselves in America.

More specifically, *Of Orphans and Warriors* explores the cultural formation of largely urban,[4] American-born Chinese in California from the time they first made their presence known in the late 1930s to the 1990s. Throughout the narrative, I privilege their thinking by using memoirs, autobiographies, and fictional writing. And in telling their stories, I am also questioning the prevailing narratives about the making of an ethnically diverse America and the analytical tools used to inform judgments ultimately about who is an American. Even as I periodize the story of Chinese America by major *events* in American history—beginning with the Japanese invasion of China in the 1930s, the World War II era, the emergence of the cold war in the 1950s, the sixties ethnic consciousness movements, and the rise of the idea of "postethnic" identity in the eighties and the nineties— I do not assume that the individual identity-making process can always be explained by structural and or ideological changes occurring over time.[5] Unlike conventional historical projects, *Of Orphans and Warriors* takes a multidisciplinary approach that is first and foremost concerned with reconstituting voices of American-born Asians rather than subsuming them under a convenient structural or chronological framework. In some cases, certain individuals threaten to break out of the very narratives that frame their stories.

I chose California as the geographic focus of this study since it has the oldest history and a consistently sizable population of American-born Chinese generations over the decades. Moreover, certain earmarks specific to California, such as the historical memory of a long and virulent anti-Chinese movement, the infamy and notoriety earned in popular literature and Hollywood films by West Coast Chinatowns, as well as the spacial and relational proximity the Chinese on the West Coast shared with Japanese Americans, make for an enlivening regional study. And yet, whenever possible, I bring in the experiences of American-born Chinese based elsewhere so as to highlight regional variations. Their differences notwithstanding, however, it must still be said that the regional study based in California, given the historical primacy of California in the making of Asian America, has broader implications for understanding the experiences of other groups. I hope that my study of Chinese Americans will inspire works that examine the experiences of other American-born populations. Comparative studies, looking at the cultural formation of American-born Asians with that of other ethnic American-born segments, such as the Jewish American, Mexican American, and postemancipation second- and third-generation African Americans, would also be fruitful venues.

"The most glaring omission," wrote the historian Sucheng Chan in the preface to *Entry Denied*, "is the absence of any essays on the second, American-born, generation . . . and the myriad, cultural, social, intergenerational, and interracial conflicts they experienced."[6] In the general literature about Asian America, the native-born population receives mention only as footnotes to the discussion of the discriminatory immigration policies against the Chinese, responsible for the tardy arrival of the second generation.

Historians Ronald Takaki, in *Strangers from a Different Shore: A History of Asian Americans* (1989), and Sucheng Chan, in *Asian America: An Interpretive History* (1991), devote several pages to the native-born Asian American experience, highlighting how being born and raised in America set them apart from the world of immigrants. Judy Yung's *Unbound Feet: A Social History of Chinese American Women in San Francisco* (1995) contains a chapter about the American daughters of immigrant women. While noting important differences between the generations and their outlooks, Yung's treatment of the second generation is limited to women and ends in the post–World War II period. Other, more comprehensive, histories of Chinese Americans, such as *Chinese Experience in America* (1989) by Henry Tsai, provide a much needed historical overview but are once again largely focused on the immigrant experience. Finally, *Claiming America: Constructing Chinese American Identities During the Exclusion Era*, a work edited by K. Scott Wong and Sucheng Chan (1998), devotes half of the book to essays about the social, cultural, and political history of the American-born generations, but its scope is limited to the pre–World War II years.[7]

————

The absence of American-born Chinese in the annals of American history can perhaps be explained in part by the fact that the stories of the second-generation ethnic subjects were deemed by scholars to be less compelling than those of immigrants, insofar as their lives were seen to follow a predictable path. My study dissects the ways in which the scholarly and the lay dominant society depicted Chinese America as much as it attempts to understand the ways in which the American-born generations saw themselves.

In the past, sociologists have tended to present the second-generation ethnic minority as the "marginal man" who, like the "tragic mulatto," is caught between opposite worlds, sandwiched between antithetical cultures, and is neither fully "ethnic" nor fully "American."[8] In light of this Americanization narrative, it comes as no surprise that the second generation is said to be consumed with desire to enter mainstream America.

Typically, traditional scholarship describes the second generation as needing to first overcome the pull from the immigrant community before it can become fully integrated into Anglo-America.[9] Seen this way, it is not white racism that prevents the second generation from achieving social and economic success in America but rather the immigrant community that poses itself as the insurmountable barrier against upward mobility. In the 1950s, Rose Hum Lee, a prominent sociologist and advocate of assimilation, implored Chinese American youths to move out of Chinatowns to free themselves from the stranglehold of the hopelessly backward immigrant Chi-

nese community. She described the second generation as caught between two cultures vying for their allegiance. This palpable tug from
both sides, Hum explained, in turn placed a considerable psychological burden on the second generation. Those American-born Chinese
who overcame the obstacles and achieved assimilation into Anglo-
America did so at a considerable price.[10]

However compelling this explanation may have been to Rose
Hum Lee and other assimilationists, my study reveals that the
Americanization thesis explains at best only partially the intricacies of
the American-born experience.[11] By privileging the voices of the
American-born Chinese themselves, I show that the second
generation's experience is a much more complicated story. The assimilationist drive was but one among many contending forces that in-
formed the identity and culture of the American-born Chinese. Even
someone who decided to become fully integrated into white America
would still make certain concessions to one's conscience, repress
aspects of one's experience, memory, and values. These were sacri-
fices of no small extent.

Jade Snow Wong, for instance, who appears in the second chapter, could be said upon first glance to be a perfect fit for the Americanization model. She received a college education unlike many of
her peers, vocally rejected Chinese patriarchy, sought employment
outside Chinatown, and eventually became an independent artist and
self-employed entrepreneur selling hand-made Chinese pottery. Yet
a closer reading of her autobiography, *Fifth Chinese Daughter* (1945),
coupled with interviews with the author, reveal that her decision to
pursue a higher education and a livelihood in America was largely
influenced by the confluence of auspicious events at the time of World
War II, when the doors of opportunity began to open for Chinese
Americans. Hence, her decision to act as the cultural bridge between
Chinese America and mainstream America was a strategic one, allowing her to make a living as an artist and entrepreneur with a Chinese flair. Before the war, Wong had thought that China held better
opportunities for her. The Americanization thesis also fails to explain why she practiced filial piety and insisted on the primacy of
her Chinese heritage and upbringing even as she embraced American

independence. Rather than suppress her ethnic difference, she chose to accentuate it.

Another reading of the second-generation experience emerges from the revisionist scholarship of the late sixties. Influenced by the civil rights and Black Power movements, which advocated ethnic pride, some scholars felt compelled to reevaluate the traditional scholarship on ethnic communities, which tended to undermine ethnicity.[12] Consequently, they emphasized ethnic retention among American-born generations rather than its loss, resistance rather than conformity to Anglicized culture. These scholars underscored the similarities between the struggles of the second generation and those of the immigrant generation. Hence they pinned ethnic identity to a set of essentialized characteristics purportedly rooted in the values and traditions of an immigrant or ethnic heritage. Accordingly, there were but two choices for the second-generation ethnic subject—conformity to mainstream America and the wholesale rejection of immigrant culture, or rebellion against the dominant culture and the adoption of immigrant culture. The second generation thus had either to conform to the ethnicity index predicated on the immigrant generation, or to seek wholesale integration into white America. Many revisionist scholars failed to see the unique position of the second generation and viewed them as mere appendages to Anglo-America or the immigrant community.

Such thinking deeply outraged some Chinese Americans who came of age in the sixties. Frank Chin, a Chinese American playwright and novelist, in his introduction to the anthology of Asian American writers *Aiiieeeee! An Anthology of Asian American Writers* (1974), rejected both Anglo-America and the foreign-born Chinese community as having anything to do with the culture and the identity of the second generation. He wrote, "America does not recognize Asian America as a presence, though Asian-Americans have been here seven generations. For seven generations we have been aware of that refusal, and internalized it, with disastrous effects."[13]

The multiculturalist paradigm that came into vogue in the 1980s and the 1990s is also inadequate to explain the second-generation conundrum. Under the unifying logic of multiculturalism, the ethnic "other" is still tied to a lasting, rich tradition, belongs to a readily identifiable sociological category, and, comparatively speaking, shares experiences and characteristics with other ethnicities similarly situated in geocultural space and history. In short, the multiculturalist approach renders the second generation all-too-familiar, passive subjects unable either to form their own identities or to bring about social change.

My research shows that in fact American-born Chinese have been active agents of history, fully capable not only of dissecting the numbing gaze of white America but also of reimagining a different place for themselves vis-à-vis Chinese America and the society at large. In listening to the voices of the American-born generations, I discern a much more complex process of negotiating identity at work. Since American-born Chinese were seen as foreigners in spite of their American-born status, how they came to forge their identities depended upon their response to the shifting currents in public opinion, which in turn was tied to the U.S.–China relations. When China was a wartime ally during World War II, Chinese were viewed as a friendly, assimilable race, but when China turned communist in 1949, the tide of public opinion turned against them. The American-born generations did not negotiate their identity, however, simply in reaction to being racialized. Other factors, such as socioeconomic status, linguistic development, personal family history, geography, educational and employment opportunity, and gender, played salient roles.

The birth of the second generation signaled for many Chinese immigrants the possibility of becoming permanent residents in America. In the hopes of planting their unspoken dreams into the American soil, Chinese immigrants welcomed the formation of families. Through their American-born progeny, immigrants could hope to rise in their socioeconomic standing and attain greater political visibility and social influence. For the Chinese, however, the American-born generations were long in the making. It would take half a century after the arrival of the first immigrants before American-born Chinese gained significant numbers. At the turn of the century, they numbered just over 9,000, 10 percent of the Chinese American population as a whole. Not until 1930 would they constitute 41 percent of the population, at 30,868. A decade later, the American-born surpassed the immigrant population for the first time, reaching 52 percent of Chinese America and numbering 40,262. In 1950, they comprised 54 percent. Only in the last two decades has the immigrant population once again become dominant, given the liberalization of immigration policy.[14] So rare were the births of Chinese babies that the Chinese newspapers faithfully printed the birth announcements. "Babies were a kind of wonder," recalled a resident in San Francisco.[15]

The rather tardy arrival of the second-generation Chinese was the result of an extremely skewed ratio between women and men. The confluence of several factors led to the scarcity of Chinese women in America. Mothers-in-law customarily kept their daughters-in-law as collateral for receiving payments from their Gold Mountain–bound sons and for their eventual return. Other cultural factors such as the Confucian ethos, which tied women to domesticity, discouraged women from traveling outside their homes, let alone crossing vast oceans and continents. Moreover, the high-risk and migratory nature of jobs such as gold mining, railroad construction, or land reclamation, discouraged the presence of women or families.[16]

But perhaps most detrimental to the formation of Chinese American families were restrictive immigration laws. At the height of the anti-Chinese movement, laws passed by Congress such as the Page Law of 1875 prevented the immigration of Chinese prostitutes. Since the burden of proof lay with the immigrant women to prove their respectability, the law, in effect, discouraged Chinese women from applying to immigrate in the first place. Then the anti-Chinese immigration law of 1882 and its subsequent restrictions virtually closed the doors to immigration on Chinese laborers and their wives until after World War II.[17] In 1890, the ratio of men to women stood at 27 to 1.[18] By 1930, Chinese men still comprised 80 percent of the Chinese American population.[19]

———

Chapter 1 begins with the 1930s, a period when American-born generations first came to ponder seriously their identity. With China coming under siege from the Japanese and America in economic depression, the American-born Chinese, finding themselves socially and economically excluded from the mainstream, felt compelled to define anew their identity and place in America. A nationwide debate on the subject of national allegiance defined not only their political positions vis-à-vis China and the United States but also their thoughts on what it meant to be of Chinese ancestry in America. Kaye Hong opted to go to China. Robert Dunn disagreed, saying that America was where his "allegiance" lay, since America was where he had learned "the principles of liberty and equality."[20] While the debate over national allegiance revealed how the American-born Chinese came to view themselves, the making of the Chinese village for the San Francisco World's Fair in 1939 showed how they consciously forged a public image of themselves for the dominant society. The American-born generations typically fashioned their identity in ways that most optimally benefited their socioeconomic and political situation. Thus Robert Dunn turned his perceived "Chineseness" into a career opportunity by grooming himself for a position as a Chinese representative at the United Nations, while the staunch Chinese nationalist Kaye Hong decided to stay in America after all, out of "practical" concern for employment.

The second chapter, spanning the World War II years, points to a shift in identity and consciousness among the American-born Chinese. As a result of China becoming an ally of the United States during the war, the Chinese were suddenly seen as more assimilable than they had been previously. Seeing the longtime hostility against the Chinese give way to a more auspicious cultural climate, some Chinese Americans, like Jade Snow Wong, Pardee Lowe, and Jadin Wong, through their words or actions helped to reinvent a view of China and its people as decidedly more modern and hence "American." The American-born generations positioned themselves strategically as ambassadors to both their parental and the dominant culture, thus explaining the American ways to their parents and interpreting the Chinese culture and civilization for white America. The emergence of Chinese nightclubs serving a predominantly white clientele was also indicative of a greater receptiveness by the dominant society toward the Chinese. Chinese American entertainers onstage widened the narrow spectrum of possibilities for Chinese Americans.

The third chapter shows how the American-born Chinese had little recourse but to prove to the larger society that they too were Americans, since China, having turned communist in 1949, made them once again suspect. Due to the "public hysteria," the editor of the *Chinese Press* warned readers that they must continue their "goodwill public relations and be on constant alert." He advised Chinese Americans to make every effort "to maintain closer contacts with Caucasian groups."[21] In order to show their loyalty to America, many renounced their Chinese citizenship, while others moved out of Chinatown into the suburbs in the hope of blending in, much in the way that the Japanese nisei (second generation) opted to disperse rather than risk returning in the postinternment years to their former ethnic enclaves.

Economic class distinction became an important factor in the way that American-born generations came to negotiate their identity at this time. Only those with financial means could move out of Chinatown. The repressive politics of McCarthyism at home, and China turning communist abroad, were factors that undoubtedly played a significant role for the way American-born Chinese chose to represent themselves to society at large. And yet Chinese Americans interpreted the Americanization process much differently than did the dominant culture. This was a period of very high acculturation but also of an equally strong sense of ethnic solidarity.

The late sixties and the seventies are the subject of the fourth chapter. It features a faction of Chinese Americans who renounced the norms and values of white society. While some American-born Chinese were content to play the "model minority," others, inspired by the civil rights and Black Power movements, as well as the antiwar movement in the late sixties, began to join in the protest against racism. For the first time, a segment of the American-born Chinese, along with other American-born Asians, pointed to the legacy of Asian presence in America in order to legitimate their political positioning as Asian Americans. With a sense of urgency, some Chinese Americans, like Frank Chin, wanted to fill in what I call the "missing content" of culture. Without the weight of history and tradition, Asian Americans flourished as cultural advance guards of Asian America. Capturing the spirit of this era, Frank Chin was said to have stated, "We've got to think up something. If we don't come up with something [referring to a distinctive Chinese or Asian American culture], we're going to make something up."[22] There was something palpably exciting about having to make things up from scratch.

Securing a distinct cultural identity translated for some into a promise of greater visibility and political leverage in a society that perceived Asians as passive and inconsequential. The notion of identity as property or emblem to mark one's status and place in society proved useful in this period of social protests. Having rejected the values, traditions, and norms of white society, some American-born Chinese felt the need to invent an identity and culture that was uniquely Chinese or Asian American. Some experimented with black culture while others acquainted themselves with the philosophy of the Chinese Red Guards. Also noteworthy were the dissenting voices of women, who expressed their refusal to fit neatly into the cultural mold shaped largely by the Asian American male leadership.

In the fifth and final chapter, I examine the exploration of ethnic identity inscribed in the writings of Chinese Americans in the eighties and nineties. While the sixties secured a common political identity for Asian Americans, Chinese Americans in the succeeding decades inherited a cultural canvas largely left unfinished. Frank Chin returns with a formula and a tradition for reconstituting Chinese American culture and identity in his didactic novel *Donald Duk* (1991). Shawn Wong also reemerges, going beyond what he calls "grandfather's stories" in *American Knees* (1995), in which the young orphaned protagonist of his earlier novel has matured into a middle-aged postethnic who is in the curious position of disinheriting his ethnicity in the dizzying age of multiculturalism. While Chin's

Donald Duk reflects upon what it means to hold on to a heritage that is clearly Chinese American, Wittman Ah Sing in Maxine Hong Kingston's *Tripmaster Monkey* (1987) contemplates the origin and meaning of racializing, and its effect on the individual person. The writings of Fae Myenne Ng and David Wong Louie bring us back to rethinking the place of American-born Asians in relation to the immigrant generation, given the changed demographics that once again place the American-born generation in the minority.

A considerable portion of the raw material for this project comes from oral history, comprised of interviews conducted by myself, as well as interviews housed at various archives. They were gleaned from oral history collections at the Hoover Institute in Stanford, The Bancroft Library and the Asian American Studies Library at the University of California at Berkeley, and the Asian American Studies Center at the University of California at Los Angeles. Since the lives of American-born Chinese have gone largely unrecorded in the history annals, oral interviews have been an indispensable resource for the study of Asian America. I also used English language newspapers written by and for the American-born generations. *Chinese Digest* and *Chinese Press* provided valuable insights into the self-identification of the American-born generations. Finally, memoirs, family histories, journals, autobiographies, and novels gave intimate views of how American-born generations thought of themselves, the America of their dreams, and their place in it.

I examined fiction, not only for its literary themes and motifs but also for its sociological context. Some might contend that very little about how an ethnic writer actually thought about identity could be gleaned from published writings intended for an audience of the broader society more often than not. One might argue that there is a difference between the way ethnic subjects projected a public self-image in these writings, as opposed to the way identity might be talked about in private writings. And yet, I would argue that, in spite of the very public nature of these writings, these were also the works of artists whose motivation to write can safely be assumed to have been inspired by more than a desire to gain acceptance among a mainstream readership. One would be hard pressed to make facile distinctions between the public and the private image of the self, as the two are dialectically related to each other. Art (as in fictional writing), after all, is about rethinking old problems through new creative forms. For a people whose identity has depended so much on their survival, the attempt to invent themselves anew was akin to art.

1

"Go West . . .

to China"

Chinese Americans
in the 1930s

The old adage, "Go West, young man," no longer becomes applicable to this American youth. . . . It is for me, "Go further west, young man. Yes, further west, across the Pacific to China.

—Kaye Hong

I owe much pride and gratitude to America for the principles of liberty and equality which it upholds for the protection of its government . . . and for its schools and institutions in which I have participated. Without them, I certainly could not be what I am now.

—Robert Dunn

"We were ghettoized within just these few square blocks," stated Thomas Chinn, who grew up in San Francisco's Chinatown during the 1930s.[1] Before World War II, the Chinese in America were a largely ignored and forgotten people. Isolated from the larger society and racially segregated, the majority of the Chinese were concentrated in urban ghettos. "We were not allowed to come out and mingle with other people outside of our community. We were too strange and were even discriminated against physically," recalled Thomas Chinn.[2] The emerging second- and third-generation

Chinese Americans, who constituted over half of the Chinese American population by the 1940s, had a status imposed by laws and various social institutions similar to that of African Americans in the South. Outside Chinatown, Chinese Americans customarily were refused service in restaurants or cafés. A Chinese American could not lawfully marry a white person. "Oriental" schools were designated for Chinese pupils; the few who attended "white" schools were prevented by racial prejudice from participating in extracurricular activities and other student organizations, as well as from using public swimming pools, other recreational facilities, and social clubs. Those who desired to play sports, to dance, or to debate had to form their own clubs.[3]

How these American-born youths came to negotiate their identity will be the focus of this chapter. I found little evidence to support the widely held assimilationist thesis, which states that second-generation members of ethnic groups historically identified with mainstream American culture and eagerly adopted and emulated its norms and values in the hope of becoming accepted. Unlike their European counterparts, who could change their last names and blend in, the American-born Chinese, by virtue of their physical appearance, had to contend with their already constituted identity firmly etched onto the minds of many Euro-Americans by both the print and visual media. The question of Chinese American identity was made all the more poignant by the fact that they were, as a rule, barred from the mainstream job market, rendered politically invisible, and socially segregated into Chinatowns. By examining and analyzing the "Great Debate of 1936" and Chinese American participation in the 1939 World's Fair, I will show the complex processes involved in the negotiation of Chinese American consciousness and identities in the 1930s.

Economic Exclusion

Exclusion from jobs was even more pronounced for the second generation of Chinese Americans, particularly during the Great Depression. American-born Chinese with college degrees and special training were largely excluded from mainstream jobs. As a result of such discrimination, along with the decline in tourist trade during the Depression, many were either unemployed or underemployed. The graduating class of 1936 at the University of California had twenty-eight American-born Chinese, many of whom had earned degrees in engineering, economics, architecture, optometry, pharmacy, and commerce.[4] Few found jobs in the fields in which they had been trained, because most firms refused to hire second-generation Chinese Americans, even if they were well educated and equipped with special talents. Nate R. White of the *Christian Science Monitor* reported a similar situation. He found that there were some five thousand young Chinese in San Francisco for whom there seemed to be "no future worthy of their skills."[5] According to the Oriental Division of the United States Employment Service in San Francisco, more than 90 percent of its placements were in the service industries, mainly in the culinary trades.[6] Instead of being employed in the areas for which they had been trained, many were carrying trays, washing dishes, cutting meat, ironing clothes, drying fish, and selling Chinese herbs.[7]

These menial jobs were demoralizing. Educated in American public schools, the American-born generation understood what were considered respectable occupations. Having grown up in Chinatown, they knew all too well that to work as a cook, a restaurateur, a laundryman, or a waiter involved long, laborious hours and little pay. A survey of Chinese high school students showed that engineering and teaching were the two most popular professional aspirations. Fewer than one percent expressed a desire to walk in the vocational footsteps of their fathers.[8] Nevertheless, many were forced to enter their parents' businesses, while some ventured to open their own small businesses in Chinatown.

The Depression heightened the economic and social isolation of the Chinese inside Chinatown. The American-born Chinese likened their situation to that of those trapped in one of those crowded, dilapidated tenements in Chinatown, without windows and with two-foot-wide hallways.[9] By 1935, contrary to the common belief that the Chinese would "take care of their own" or that they had a special talent for silently enduring hardship, more than 350 families in San Francisco's Chinatown were receiving assistance from the San Francisco Relief Administration.[10] Rodney Chow of Los Angeles remembered how no one gave out "lei see"—money wrapped in red pouches—on the Chinese New Year during the years of the Depression. His family was so poor that they slept on the floor. The only pieces of furniture Chow recalled seeing were a few wooden stools and a table. Soda crackers and water with an occasional boiled head of lettuce with soy sauce typified suppers in Chow's household.[11] A survey of 119 of the families receiving relief aid showed that there were on average 2.2 persons to a room, only 40 families with private kitchens, and 25 with private bathing facilities.[12] Memories of living in Apartment #301 remained vivid for David Gan of San Francisco:

> It had two rooms and a closet-sized kitchen with a window facing other apartments. George and I slept on a sofa bed. Ma and Pa slept in the bedroom with Virginia, Norman and Hank, I think. The dimly lit and narrow hallway had brown linoleum and I rode my tricycle at times. There was no bathroom. Each floor had a communal bathroom, consisting of a tub and a toilet, shared by four or five apartments' tenants.[13]

Fu Manchu versus Charlie Chan

In addition to social isolation and economic deprivation, Chinese Americans also suffered from demeaning popular images. The American-born Chinese protested the representation of the Chinese as Fu Manchu, "the sleepy celestial enveloped in mists of opium fumes," or "the long-fingered Mandarins chasing sing-song girls at chop suey joints." Speaking for many, the editor of the *Chinese Digest* stated, "We are tired of comedies."[14]

A creation of the British author Sax Rohmer, Fu Manchu was the embodiment of the "Yellow Peril." Almost all of Rohmer's forty-one novels, as well as a significant collection of his short stories, postulated that yellow hordes were on the verge of sweeping the world. Fu Manchu's bizarre assassination schemes and his other unusual cruelties epitomize the image of Asian threat to the West.[15] His horrid actions are matched only by his physical appearance, as described by the author himself:

> Imagine a person, tall, lean and feline, high-shouldered with a brow like Shakespeare and a face like Satan, a close-shaven skull, and long magnetic eyes of true cat-green. Invest him with all the cruel cunning of an entire Eastern race, accumulated in one giant intellect, with all the resources, if you will, of a wealthy government, which, however, already has denied all knowledge of his existence. Imagine that awful being, and you have a mental picture of Dr. Fu-Manchu, the yellow peril incarnate in one man.[16]

If Fu Manchu was the paragon of Chinese evil, then Charlie Chan was the model of the friendly Chinese. Film scholar Dorothy Jones confirmed that John Stone, the producer of the original Charlie Chan films at Fox Studios, saw the characterization of Charlie Chan "as a refutation of the unfortunate Fu Manchu characterization of the Chinese."[17] Devoid of any assertiveness and sexuality, Charlie Chan is self-effacing to a fault. Typically, he says things like "I am so sorry. I have made stupid error. Captain—is it possible you will ever forgive me?"[18]

Charlie Chan, the creation of Earl Derr Biggers, who wrote six Charlie Chan novels between 1925 and 1932, was a benign, overweight detective who spoke "pidgin" English peppered with pseudo-Confucian aphorisms: "The Emperor Shi Hwang-ti, who built the Great Wall of China, once said: He who squanders today talking of yesterday's triumph, will have nothing to boast of tomorrow."[19] Unlike Fu Manchu, however, Chan was on the side of the law, solving murder mysteries with his uncanny intellect. The stories were serialized in *The Saturday Evening Post*, published as books, and appeared in forty-eight feature films.[20]

Scientific and academic institutions also created an image of the Chinese as decidedly strange and peculiar. A Works Progress Administration (WPA) task force purportedly aimed at examining health-related issues of Chinese Americans in San Francisco's Chinatown turned it into an ethnographic spectacle. Photographs marked with measurements of Chinese American children's heads, faces, and body stature, along with samples of their hair, were sent to museums all across the country. Alfred Louis Kroeber of the University of California at Berkeley and Allen Danforth of Stanford University, key scientists behind the study, sought to establish a classification for the physical racial type of the Chinese.[21]

Louise Chin related a "humiliating" incident she endured as a result of such studies. She was made to stand in front of her second-grade class as a "specimen" when her class was studying China. Chin related how her teacher used her as a model to point out all the characteristics of the Chinese: "There were the slant, almond eyes, the black hair—coarse and straight, you notice, don't you, class? The nose that was practically no nose, the cheekbones and the general blank look."[22] Actually, her "blank look," Chin explained, "concealed a wealth of emotions underneath."[23]

Chinese as the Humble and Gentle People

Another prevailing stereotype was that of a humble, gentle people. The wide popularity of a novel by Pearl S. Buck, *The Good Earth* (1931), was largely responsible for a more humane characterization of the Chinese. The novel follows the story of a Chinese peasant and his wife who struggle against natural disasters, political turmoil, and human cruelty. The couple, however, persevere and do not forsake their lives, which are rooted in the soil. At a time when Americans were struggling during the Depression, many people easily identified with the protagonists of *The Good Earth*. Also, at a time when China was receiving much news coverage because of the Sino-Japanese War, the American public, moved by the portrayal of the Chinese characters in the novel, came to view the Chinese as a brave and noble people, unjustly attacked by the cruel Japanese. Harold Isaacs has argued that Buck's book became the single most powerful force in garnering national sympathy for the Chinese during the Sino-Japanese War.[24] The John Day Company's many editions and renditions sold more than two million copies. In 1937, an extraordinarily popular film based on the novel was seen by some twenty-three million Americans.[25]

The Great Debate of the 1930s

Given the plethora of stereotypical depictions of the Chinese, the American-born generations became all the more eager to define for themselves who they were and what it meant to be Chinese American. A national debate on the future of Chinese born in America set the stage for doing just that.

The Ging Hawk Club—a women's social club based in New York—in 1936 sponsored a national essay competition: "Does My Future Lie in China or America?" "In America lies my future," answered Robert Dunn at the beginning of his first-prize-winning essay. Kaye Hong, a second-place winner, expressed the opposite view, that his future lay in China. "The old adage, 'Go West, young man,' no longer becomes applicable to this American youth. It is for me, 'Go further west, young man. Yes, further west, across the Pacific to China.'"[26]

The publication of these two essays in the *Chinese Digest* opened a national debate on the future of the Chinese who had been born in America. What began as a friendly writing contest turned into a verbal battle. Letters flowed in from across the country. Dunn's position favoring a future in America seemed less than appealing to his American-born peers. The Chinese Students' Club at Stanford University became Dunn's main opponents. The Stanford students wrote in the section of the paper appropriately labeled "Firecrackers" that Mr. Dunn was "unwise," if not outright "unpatriotic" to China. The ideological war between Dunn and his opponents raged for months.[27]

In the debate, two positions became clear—one expressing allegiance to China, the other, to America. Actually, this debate revealed much more than the writers' political positions. Behind the authors' political or ideological consciousness lay certain basic assumptions about how they perceived their ethnic or national identity. From the ensuing debate, we can say that there were two positions, one advocating a future in China and the other in America. Dunn advocated allegiance to America and emphasized its members' Americanness. Kaye Hong and the Stanford students, in contrast, favored a future in China and felt culturally closer to things Chinese. By taking their political views into the public arena, both groups made positive assertions about what it meant to be Chinese in America.

Robert Dunn, who grew up in Roxbury, Massachusetts, was at the time an undergraduate at Harvard University. Although he had not grown up in a large Chinese community, he claimed that his upbringing was very Chinese. By his own assertion, Dunn was "radical" and "unconventional." His thinking was radical, he said, because in choosing America over China he broke away from the views of the parental generation, whose members encouraged loyalty and service to China. "Ever since I can remember, I have been taught," wrote Dunn, "by my parents, by my Chinese friends, and by my teacher in Chinese school, that I must be patriotic to China." He was made to feel "obliged to render service to China." Breaking away from this expectation constituted a "radical" move, demonstrating an "unconventionality" with regard to Chinese norms.[28]

He related that his parents wondered how it was possible for their son to be loyal to America, a country where "the Chinese are mocked at, trodden upon, disrespected, and even spit upon." For any Chinese to desire a future in such a country would only amount to "losing face." Dunn, however, defied parental advice and decided to make his future in America. The crucial factor for Dunn was his love for what he called "American" values and principles, which he preferred to "Chinese" ways and thought. After all, he had learned "to live by Christian ideals, by liberal attitudes, and by an optimistic outlook on life." Dunn saw these principles as the very fabric of America. "I owe much pride and gratitude to America for the principles of liberty and equality which it upholds for the protection of its government . . . and for its schools and institutions in which I have participated. Without them, I certainly could not be what I am now."[29]

Dunn could not imagine how he could survive in China. He felt that there he could not make many friends who would share his values. "I shall be able to make few close relationships with the young men and women of China," Dunn decided, "for their background is of utilitarian ideals, conservative attitudes, and of a fatalistic outlook upon life." For Dunn, the "Chinese" and the "American" ways were irreconcilable.

Although he recognized that there was racism in America, Dunn believed that Chinese Americans could still successfully make a living here. "The color line," he wrote, "does not entirely prevent the American-born Chinese from getting jobs. . . . It cannot be said, therefore, that it is impossible for Chinese American youths to obtain remunerative positions in either China or America." In fact, he found that being Chinese at times worked to his favor. His experience at Harvard University was that the white students gave him "more respect" because he was Chinese. "Whatever I do in school and college in the way of extracurricular activities or of attaining high grades, I am given much more credit and popularity than an American would receive, if he did the same things," he argued. Hence, "being a Chinese among American friends" was, according to Dunn, "a sort of advantage"(3).

The Stanford students' main argument against Dunn was that he did not see the pervasiveness of racism and its damaging effects on the Chinese. They wrote, "Can racial prejudice disappear in America in a few years? When you [Dunn] fail to take cognizance of these facts in your essay, you cannot blame us for accusing you of lack of information."[30] Kaye Hong, a second-place winner who had grown up in San Francisco and attended the University of Washington in Seattle, agreed that his patriotism toward China had been shaped by his awareness of racism in America against the Chinese. Hong found the ideals propounded by American Christian democracy "hypocritical." For instance, he discovered that the principle of "equal opportunity" did not apply to the Chinese. Hong wrote, "I have learned to acknowledge that the better jobs are not available to me and that the advancement of my career is consequently limited in this fair land." Hong stated that the call to "make the world safe for democracy" left him "coldly unresponsive." Hong's patriotism was of a "different hue and texture," one "built on the mound of shame." "The ridicule heaped upon the Chinese race has long fermented within my soul," Hong explained.[31]

Hong's patriotism toward China was a product of his upbringing. Growing up in San Francisco's Chinatown, a place founded on a long history of white racism, Hong, along with many other young American-born Chinese, was constantly reminded of racial injustice in America. For others, the decision to go to China was one based on concern about employment. James Low, for instance, had always believed that going to work in China was preferable to getting a degree in engineering or anything else, since a degree hardly guaranteed a job in the United States. His father had urged him always to go to China: "Father used to tell me, 'Look at your boss, he was going to be an engineer, look what happened to him! What are you studying engineering for?'"[32]

Thomas Chinn also was trained from an early age to think about a future in China. In preparation for such an outcome, he studied the Chinese language and received a Chinese education. As the oldest son, he was sent to China in 1924 to get a "genuine" Chinese education, a practice common at the time. Such preparation grew out of his parents' fear that "if things became worse [anti-Chinese racism] they might be forced to return to China." Particularly after China became a republic in 1912, Chinese parents hoped that their children would have a future in rebuilding China. Such a life seemed more promising than working as waiters, dishwashers, or janitors in America.[33]

Indeed, the insurmountable barrier of the color line made it nearly impossible for the American-born generations to hope for an equal opportunity in America. Because of their race, many were barred from entering the mainstream labor market. Some states, including California, legislated against the employment of Chinese Americans in certain fields such as law, medicine, financial administration, dentistry, veterinary science, liquor store ownership, architecture, engineering, and realty, among others. More subtle forms of discrimination also existed. Some jobs, for instance, required union membership, a stipulation that automatically precluded the Chinese, who were barred from joining. Furthermore, the seniority system sanctioned the practice of hiring the Chinese last and firing them first.[34]

Census records indicate that during much of the 1920s and 1930s, a great majority of the gainfully employed Chinese in the United States were classified as working in domestic and personal service occupations. Chinese were listed as servants and laundry workers more than in any other class of work. According to the 1930 census, of the 19,470 Chinese American males in California above the age of ten who were gainfully employed, 7,773 were in domestic and personal service. Among these, nearly 1,000 did laundry work and 4,774 did domestic work. Others worked as barbers, chambermaids, janitors, elevator operators, and bellboys. Opportunities for women were even slimmer: fewer than 1,000 were gainfully employed.[35]

The chances for finding employment in the field of their chosen study were slight for those American-born Chinese who remained in America. Sam Lee, who headed the Asian branch of the California State Employment Service, stated, "The only Chinese ever to obtain a doctor's degree in architecture at Berkeley is glad to work in a barbecue stand." Lee also told about an electrical engineer resorting to shopkeeping in Chinatown, and a young man with a master's degree in journalism chauffeuring a rich woman.[36] In yet another case, a graduate of a recognized school of mechanical engineering had been working in a steel mill for nine years. His education far surpassed that of his American coworkers. Yet, one by one his coworkers were promoted, while he had received only small increases in salary. A draftsman when he first entered, he remained a draftsman after nine long years.[37]

Ben Fee had a different response to racism. Rather than opting to go to China, he felt that he could better serve his fellow Chinese Americans by helping them to get organized as a labor force. He belonged to a minority faction in Chinatown who saw how racism was linked to American capitalism. As a young man he drew inspiration from writings by Marx and Lenin. Among his numerous accomplishments was the establishment of the Chinese Workers' Mutual Aid Organization. Born to a mother who was known as a "bomb thrower" back in her village and a father who was a "draft-dodger," Ben was destined to be a revolutionary. As a teenager he formed the Chinese Students Club to attract like-minded youth to help him unionize laborers. Fee explained that while communism was not popular among the old guard, the younger generation was at least open to learning about it. If they tended to shy away from openly embracing socialist thinking, it was because there were some serious repercussions. Fee himself faced grave consequences for his socialist views. Reading Lenin while he was peeling potatoes cost him his job: "As I was reading that book, the doctor comes in and he says, 'What's that you're reading?' and when I say 'Cookbook,' he says, 'You don't have to look at a cookbook to peel potatoes.' So he grabs hold of me and that's the end of my job."[38]

Economic Opportunities in China

While the exclusion of Chinese from American mainstream labor helped to "push" some American-born Chinese toward China, certain factors in China also worked to "pull" them there. War-torn China, eager to rebuild, advertised its need for American-trained workers. An advertisement in *Chinese Digest* announced that the Shanghai Aviation Association was anxious to contact Chinese students of aviation in America.[39] The Chinese embassy in Washington, D.C., relayed the message that the Ministry of Industry in China had requested that engineers specializing in iron and steel smelting apply for positions in Shanghai. The Department of Agriculture disseminated the news that the Chinese government would grant money, land, and machinery to Chinese farmers trained in the United States and willing to work in China.[40]

This advertising campaign must have been effective, since it succeeded in luring an estimated 20 percent of the American-born Chinese to China in the 1930s.[41] Going to China was actually an old phenomenon. By the mid-thirties, some Chinese Americans had established themselves quite comfortably in China. Dr. Charles R. Shepherd, the Presbyterian minister at the mission church in Chinatown, wrote in an interview in *Chinese Digest* that Lai Sun of California had found a position with Texaco Company in Hong Kong, and Agnes Mark, a Canadian, worked as a secretary at the Shanghai Hospital. The full report contained an extensive list of names and occupations. Most jobs were in engineering, medicine, teaching, and research.[42]

Between 1920 and 1924, there were 2,510 more who departed for China than entered the United States. In 1931, while only 1,365 entered the United States, a greater number—3,386—left for China. Over 10,000 more Chinese left the United States than entered in the period between 1909 and 1932.[43]

The decision to go to China was influenced as much by the experience of racial prejudice as it was by practical concerns for finding employment. Kaye Hong was representative of those whose desire to go to China was ideologically motivated by his recognition of systemic and institutional racism against the Chinese in the United States. As long as racism against the Chinese existed in America, he felt, he would not be able to live and work in America. For Thomas Chinn and James Low, however, going to China had more to do with practical concerns for employment. Grace Lee Boggs, who did not go to China until she was in her seventies, explained that when she was growing up, "goingback" was spoken as a single word because it was such a common phenomenon.[44]

And yet in the 1930s, the talk of "going back" to China carried nationalist overtones. Many of the second-generation Chinese Americans understood that as long as China remained subjugated by the Japanese, prejudice would continue to depress their social and economic standing in the United States. A University of California student at Berkeley stated, "Henceforth we who are in America must lend all our efforts to the up-building of a strong united front, for the better development of the movement for national liberation in China."[45] Those who advocated a future in China tended to emphasize collective purpose rather than personal satisfaction. One student wrote, "May we unite for teamwork and be proud of our country [China]."[46] Another echoed, "It is not so much a question of the individual as it is that of the country's welfare."[47] Kaye Hong wrote, "I merely intend to become a good citizen of the great Republic, I shall support the nationalist government which is now gaining strength with each succeeding day. I shall accept the national policies as being the best moves for China. As a whole, I shall place the welfare of the nation above my own."[48] While those who advocated a future in America spoke much more about individual concerns, placing personal happiness above any national or group interest, the China advocates placed greater emphasis on the moral imperative to rebuild China.

That the China advocates identified with China was evidenced in the language used to talk about it. They used the phrase "return to China" or "going back" even though they had never been there. Denying America, their birthplace, they adopted China as their surrogate homeland. When Hong wrote "in our own country," he was referring to China, not to the United States.

Those foreseeing a future in China saw themselves as "pioneers of a new frontier"—a frontier in China. Kaye Hong best exemplified this sentiment: "It will take hundreds of thousands, millions of young men with vision to build for the future. To start the wheels of industries, to weave a cobweb or railroads and highways across the expanse of all Cathay, to advocate, to send out a fleet of trading vessels, to develop the internal resources to build a richer life for one and all."[49] Another student had a similar vision: "Great highway systems will appear all over the country, linked with an efficient railroad net. Mines will be opened and rivers harnessed for power development and flood control, streaming lines of trucks will move rapidly from city to city."[50] Given their conscious efforts to identify with China rather than with America, it is ironic that they expressed a vision similar to the miracle of industrialization found in late-nineteenth-century America. This reveals that in spite of their anti-American rhetoric, their thoroughly Eurocentric education made their notions of economic progress and modernization a vision predicated on the historical narratives of Euro-America.

Japan Symbolizes Racial Oppression

China came to symbolize a haven for a racism-free life. Only Japan threatened to spoil this dream. In the eyes of the American-born Chinese, Japan's imperialist aggression against China paralleled that of America's discrimination against Chinese Americans. During a march protesting Japanese actions in China, one student waved a placard emblazoned with the slogan "Racial Freedom and Liberty Forever!"[51] For this student, as for many other people, the struggle against Japanese imperialism in China went hand in hand with the fight against racism in America. Thus, Japan, as the identifiable, common enemy, came to represent more than just an aggressor nation against China; it became the incarnation of racial oppression itself.

Sometimes protests against the Japanese required a good deal of imagination. Ben Fee described convincing Chinese American women from the National Dollar Store to foil plans for the welcoming of a delegation of Japanese officials that included the presentation of keys to the city. Ben Fee explained how he deflected attention from the Japanese officials: "The women wore slit skirts of colorful silk. They looked just like *Flower Drum Song* girls. They were holding slogans, not ordinary, but colorful and embroidered, saying things like 'Down with Japanese Aggression.' The police don't know what to do with them. You can't hit those ladies." Not surprisingly, the delegation left San Francisco in a hurry, hoping to find a better reception in Seattle.[52]

Young second-generation Chinese grew up with the idea that Japan, along with Britain and America, was the imperialist enemy of China. James Low recalled acquiring his political consciousness in the Chinese-language schools. "Ever since I was small, the Japanese had been committing aggression in China." The Chinese school principal "was always attacking Chiang Kai-shek for not fighting the Japanese." Many of his Chinese teachers were always talking about "imperialism and prejudice, and how imperialism was the cause of China's downfall, how the British forced opium on the Chinese, et cetera, et cetera, and that the Chinese don't have a chance here." Although he did not always understand what was going on, by the "demonstrations and parades" and "speeches on the playground" he "kind of got the feeling" that he did not have a "Chinaman's chance" of making it in America.[53]

At the Chinese Young People's Summer Conference that took place at Lake Tahoe in 1935, when the question of the future was

raised, the balloting showed that 75 percent of the participants favored a future in China. Many insisted that second-generation Chinese *must* go back to China.[54] The prevailing desire among the
American-born to establish their future in China took on a symbolic
significance and laid the foundation for a nationalistic/separatist ideology. Much like the mid-nineteenth-century Pan-Africanists led by
Martin Delany, Paul Cuffe, and others, and that of the earlier part of
the twentieth century led by Marcus Garvey, some Chinese Americans in the 1930s advocated going back to China as a protest against
American racism. While there were considerable differences between
the two communities, such as the absence of charismatic leaders in
the Chinese American community who could galvanize a movement
in the way black leaders like Garvey were able to do, still Chinese
Americans shared with African Americans the belief that there would
not be a time in the near future when Chinese Americans would be
considered equals with white Americans. "All of us back in those
days had thought of going back," recalled Rodney Chow, a longtime
resident of Los Angeles. Racism, in his opinion, fueled the desire to
go to China:

> We had never felt that we were Americans. And we never felt
> that we were Americans because there was a very deep hatred
> for the Caucasian people. The hatred was thrown on us and it
> was reciprocated back to them. We never referred to ourselves
> as "Americans," we referred to ourselves as "Chinese," even
> though many of us had difficulty speaking Chinese. . . . We al-
> ways said we would go to China, go back to China.[55]

The discrepancy between thinking and practice indicated that
life in China perhaps had its difficulties too. Immigration records
show that, perhaps as a result of the favorable relations between China
and the United States just prior to and during World War II, many
Chinese Americans returned to the United States from China. Between 1940 and the start of the war, many American-born Chinese
came back to the United States in hope of a better life. The sudden
swelling in the number of Chinese being admitted into the United
States from China indicates that a good percentage of those entering

the United States were Chinese American returnees. The number being admitted into the United States from China rose sharply beginning in 1940, with 920 entering. In 1941, 1,003 entered, compared to 231 in 1934 and 297 in 1936. This shift suggests a reversal of the trend of the preceding two decades, which showed far larger numbers departing for China than vice versa.[56] "I was disillusioned after a few months," said a young engineer. "First of all, I found that I did not master the Chinese language and the upside down Cantonese that I had learned in those afternoon classes on Stockton Street only evoked hilarity over there." Besides, he discovered, he could not learn anything new in his field because his American training made him far superior to his Chinese colleagues.[57] Others complained about the "filth and poverty of the Chinese villages," which appeared to be "worse off than Chinatown."[58] To do well in China, one had to be fully fluent in Chinese and have a marketable skill. In addition, it helped to have connections with influential persons. Thomas Chinn, like some others, went to China in 1933—in his case, with hopes of opening up a sporting goods shop. He returned when his business venture failed.[59]

In the end, Kaye Hong and Robert Dunn both had experiences opposite to those they had envisioned. Hong remained in the United States. When I last spoke to him, he was a retired businessman living in San Francisco. When I asked why he decided to stay, he answered, "It was actually harder to find a good position in China, unless you had connections. Although in my heart, I wanted to serve China, practical circumstances—such as meeting my wife, getting married, and starting a family—led me to stay in America working at whatever odd jobs I could find to support my family."[60]

Ironically, it was Robert Dunn who went to China for a while after working with the Chinese United Nations delegation to help frame the UN Charter. He married a woman born and raised in China. After the communists occupied the Chinese mainland, he and his wife came back to the United States and took up residence in Maryland.[61] Fortunately for Dunn, he had connections to high officials in China who offered him a position he found "hard to pass up." Much to his surprise, his stay in China was a "pleasant" one. He made friends with Chinese people whose values and ways of thinking were similar to those in the West. When asked why he had gone to China, he answered that although he is "bicultural" he had always considered himself "first and foremost a Chinese."[62]

Dunn and Hong shared some deep-rooted similarities. Whether they felt greater loyalty to China or America, they could not escape the fact that they felt more Chinese. Identifying with Chinese culture had more to do with feelings that emerged from their marginalized status in American society than with any education in, familiarity with, or expertise in classical Chinese art, history, or literature. Hong, having grown up in San Francisco, could hardly walk away unscathed by a long and virulent legacy of racism against the Chinese; Dunn, brought up in rural Massachusetts, safely removed from anti-Chinese sentiment, was understandably more optimistic about his prospects in America. Dunn was not, however, blind to the existence of racism. What both Dunn and Hong wanted was to be freed from the shadow of the "ancient glories" of the Chinese cultural past. In spite of what his parents had told him, Hong stated, "We, the younger generation, have nothing to be proud of except the time-worn accomplishments of our ancient ancestors."[63] Similarly, the constant harping by Dunn's parents urging that he "should be proud of China's four thousand years of glorious and continuous history" left him "unmoved."[64] Hong and Dunn both knew that no matter how glorious China's past had been, China in the present was seen by the United States as a weakling nation, economically destitute, socially backward, and politically impotent. They were convinced that they, the Chinese living in America, would be more respected if modern-day China were stronger.

There were two ways to achieve this end. Dunn's solution was to stay in America and become a goodwill "ambassador": "Serve China by building up a good impression of the Chinese among Americans, by spreading good-will and clearing up misunderstandings, by interesting the Americans in the Chinese through personal contacts."[65] In contrast, Hong thought that it would be better to physically build up China with hammer and nail. "Then and only then," claimed Hong, "can the present generation of Chinese really save their faces."[66] "While China's industries are unborn, her resources yet underground, and her people jobless and starving, the present generation of American-born Chinese cannot save their faces."[67] As long as China remained subjugated by the Japanese, Dunn and Hong believed, along with many other young Chinese Americans, their economic as well as social status would suffer.[68]

Ultimately, the American-born Chinese hoped for an America free of racism. "As long as the 'bok gwais' [literally translated as "white devils"] ruled over America," a young man explained, "the possibility of a happy life in America was just a dream."[69] America as such would be a place the Chinese could claim as their own; what better way was there to claim America than to have it be discovered by a Chinese? One can imagine the surprise and delight of American-born Chinese when they heard about *Steel of Empire*, written by a Canadian, John Murray Gibbon, who claimed that there was "sufficient data to prove that a Chinese Buddhist monk [Hui Sien] was really the very first discoverer of America" a thousand years before Columbus and about five hundred years before Erikson. A favorable review of this book by William Hoy received four full columns in the book section of *Chinese Digest*. However remote the possibility, it must have appealed to some American-born Chinese who, upon reading this, began to entertain extravagant notions of claiming America as their own—even if the possibility seemed dream-years away.[70]

The 1939 World's Fair

Although achieving equality seemed difficult, Chinese Americans seized what opportunities there were for enhanced well-being. Some believed that reforming the general image of Chinatown would help to improve the way they were viewed. When the 1939 World Fair came to San Francisco, Chinese Americans had their chance to implement these reforms. Eager to shed the "sordid aspects of the old Chinatown," *Chinese Digest* editorialized, many American-born Chinese hoped to "modernize" Chinatown in preparation for the World's Fair. The event offered them an opportunity to re-create their town. They were tired of the age-old tales, in popular literature from the late nineteenth century through the 1940s, depicting Chinatown as the abode of mysterious Chinese, as a place where horrible crimes were perpetrated, where so-called hatchet men killed one another at the slightest provocation, where vices were indulged in by both Chinese and unfortunate Caucasians who were lured into its "dens of iniquity," and where "every almond-eyed girl who peeps out from a tenement house window at the passing throng was a sing-song girl."[71] The editorial in the *Digest* lamented that "no people in America were more misunderstood than the Chinese." It blamed "the pulp magazines and Hollywood" for keeping "this illusion alive."[72]

The tourist trade had also been built up on these exotic fantasies. Sightseers by the tens of thousands thronged the streets of Chinatown to see the "Oriental" iniquities and mysteries. In fact, the tourist industry perpetuated these racist images of the Chinese by disseminating sensational tales, which the tourists then spread. Compared to these disparaging stereotypes, Pearl S. Buck's image of the Chinese as humble and gentle people was preferred. Chinese Americans enthusiastically applauded Buck's image over the negative, sensationalized ones, in the hopes of being better received by the larger society.[73]

"We look forward to the time when our own generation will sponsor some projects for the coming San Francisco Exposition which will be remunerative to us and educational to the public," editorialized *Chinese Digest*.[74] This hopeful prediction would become a reality. The World's Fair allowed the Chinese Americans to refurbish Chinatown as well as to build a model Chinatown on the fair grounds proper. The fair's directors offered to put up $1,200,000 to build a Chinese Village on Treasure Island occupying more than a city block of space. Many American-born Chinese marveled at this opportunity to build an ideal Chinatown, a Chinatown of their dreams, to serve as a model and inspiration for the real Chinatown on Grant Avenue. The leadership in the planning committee was composed largely of American-born Chinese and Chinese-born merchants. Ching Wah Lee, who served as an editor for *Chinese Digest*, and George Jue, another American-born community activist, were the main leaders of Chinese Factors Inc., the planning committee. Representing the interests of the American-born, they were careful to emphasize "genuine" Chinese expressions instead of re-creating the falsified, tourist-trap inventions that had inundated parts of Chinatown. When certain members of the merchant class, whose primary interest had always been financial profit, suggested that they add nude girls jumping out of cakes as a tourist attraction, the leadership of Chinese Factors Inc. protested, reasoning that it would be both "tasteless" and "not Chinese." The Reverend Edwar Lee, who was tangentially involved with the fair, recalled that there were many such arguments between the merchant class and the American-born Chinese. "The merchants were primarily interested in profits," stated the Reverend Lee, "whereas the American-born Chinese wanted to do things with more integrity."[75]

In their efforts to reform Chinatown, these young Chinese Americans sought to change the very premise of tourism as it had come to be known in Chinatown. Tourism would be no longer a thrill show, but an educational experience. The tourist would learn about China and Chinese culture by being exposed to genuine expressions of things Chinese. The underlying principle behind the effort to reform Chinatown architecturally was this motto: "If we must modernize Chinatown, do it. But do it by using Chinese forms and color as a basis for this development."[76] Crucially, China, not Chinese America, was to be the source from which the cultural and aesthetic adornment of Chinatown were to be derived.

When the World Fair Chinese Village was finished, Chinese Factors Inc. and others involved were sure they had been successful in their aim. Approximately a million visitors entered the Chinese Village, through a towering gateway that mimicked the Peking Palace entrance. Once inside, they encountered a Mandarin theater, a Home of Fortune, a temple, a cocktail lounge, and many ships displaying Cathay's arts and handicrafts made by indigenous Chinese artisans. In addition, the crowds were delighted by a beautiful willow tea house and a Chinese garden. In the background stood a 130–foot-tall pagoda, which held a formidable collection of Chinese art, including jade carvings, tapestries, and paintings from ancient China.[77] David Gan remembered the pride he felt visiting the fairgrounds and seeing the Chinese Village done up in black, crimson, and gold; he thought it the most colorful part of the fair.[78]

To cap it all, the fair opened with a Chinese New Year's parade, since the New Year fell on February 19, a day after the fair's opening. Two monstrous dragons, each four hundred feet long, one gold and the other silver, led the procession. Like everything else, these dragons were designed and assembled by skilled artists and craftsmen in China. Adding to the fanfare, the Chinese YMCA Bugle and Drum Corps led the parade for the Exposition.[79]

Less spectacular, but valued for being "genuinely" Chinese, was a re-created Chinese farming village that represented village life in interior China. Within the village were a typical farmer using an old wooden plow drawn by a water buffalo, a village temple, and a small shop where craftsmen sold their goods. Even the topsoil was imported from China. Chinese Factors Inc. called this farming village the Good Earth Settlement, after Pearl S. Buck's novel. While the actual village settlement bore little resemblance to the farming village described in the novel, the connection was obvious; both the novel and the settlement served to humanize the Chinese, showing them to be hardworking peasants.[80]

Back in the actual Chinatown, on Grant Avenue, Chinese businessmen refurbished their stores in Chinese colors and constructed modern bars and coffee shops, which began to attract more visitors. Chinatown acquired a new image. It was no longer an alien world teeming with vice and intrigue, fit only for the wild or the criminal at heart, but a safe, educational, and colorful place fit for all. David Gan and his brother, George, benefited from the resurgence of tourism.

> We went into a family business selling Chinese candy to the tourists who visited Chinatown. We started by sitting at the concrete flower bed curb in front of Old St. Mary's Church on Grant Avenue and California Street. . . . Then George and I traversed our side of Grant Avenue and asked tourists to buy the candy. Sales were much improved by this direct contact approach. On a good day, we both sold ten dollars gross and it was good money those days.[81]

By the late 1930s, many once-failing businesses were able to rebound from the economic depression. As the tourist trade began to pick up, the Chinese import business, which had declined precipitously since 1931, recovered by 1935. George Jue, the managing director of Chinese Factors, Inc., reported in 1939, "Chinatown is enjoying the biggest business boom in a decade."[82] In 1938, tourism in Chinatown increased to an annual value of $5 million.[83] In addition, two hundred new jobs were created at the fairground as well as fifty in Chinatown, particularly for young women who served as hostesses, secretaries, cigarette girls, and waitresses.[84] Even after the fair, tourism did not decline, and the American-born generations continued their efforts to improve Chinatown's image.

American-born Chinese saw the fair, however, as more than simply an opportunity for employment or increased earnings. By examining the process by which the American-born generations attempted to shape a new image of themselves for the wider public, we get a rare glimpse into the cultural politics of Chinese American identity in pre–World War II America. Motivated by the hope of winning greater acceptance and respect from the dominant society, American-born Chinese carefully crafted a self-image antithetical to the negative portrayal of the Chinese as a morally decadent and barbarous people. To counteract the prejudice they encountered, the American-born generations invented themselves in the image of the "genuine" Chinese, as if they had acquired a pipeline transference of culture from ancient China. Above all else, the American-born Chinese, motivated by the desire to present themselves in a favorable light so as to curb the racial prejudice against them, designed the Chinese segment of the World's Fair to achieve this end.

This insistence on displaying genuine expressions of things "Chinese"—even to the point of importing the topsoil of the Chinese Village from China—is evidence of their need to authenticate the "truthful" version of Chinese America as opposed to the "false" Hollywood representations of them. Still, by making a positive assertion about what constitutes Chineseness, they were complicit in objectifying the Chinese. Also noteworthy is the sheer absence of any discussion about claiming a "Chinese American" heritage and identity in either the planning of the fair or the actual building of the Chinese Village. Their failure to assert any linkage to Chinese America certainly was not due to any historical blindness. Rather, their move "to go back to China" in the hopes of retrieving an identity and a culture hitherto eclipsed by Hollywood was for the American-born generation the most viable and enabling act of self-assertion possible at the time, given that they lived in a society that simply could not see the Chinese—even those born in America—as "American." While the American-born generations could not wholly escape internalizing their otherness, they remade themselves in ways that challenged and subverted the stereotypical rendition of the Chinese.

Conclusion

In the period before World War II, Chinatowns such as the one in San Francisco were self-contained neighborhoods equipped not only with Chinese restaurants, "Oriental" schools, and herb shops, but with opera houses also. Aside from the tourist industry, the residents had little day-to-day contact with members of the dominant society. Many young American-born Chinese, far from being full of assimilationist desire, saw themselves primarily as "Chinese" and kept to themselves. Their ethnic identification and solidarity were less the result of making choices based on a knowledge of things Chinese than the consequence of a lack of choices, given the social and economic isolation imposed on them by the larger society. Robert Dunn's loyalty to America was a minority viewpoint. Not until World War II, when the American public had come to view the Chinese as a friendly race, did Chinese Americans in larger numbers adopt a loyalist stance toward America. In the 1930s, even as some protested their parents' imposition of traditional Chinese conventions, institutional and societal racism caused them to feel "un-American." They had little choice except to identify themselves as "Chinese." In short, their self-identification as "ethnic" in the 1930s was predicated on their awareness of their social, economic, and political marginalization vis-à-vis the broader society. Even though a great majority of American-born generations had arguably acculturated to the norms of mainstream America, only a few believed that assimilation into its sociocultural matrix was truly possible. While a spectrum of identities could be said to exist in the prewar years, the debate on the future of Chinese Americans and the Chinese contribution to the World Fair, among other things, point to an emergent nationalist consciousness in the American-born generations of the 1930s.

2

"Bridging

the Gap"

Cultural Interpreters of
the World War II Era

We occupy a most unique position standing betwixt the cultures and traditions of our forefathers and that of the land of our birth.
—*Lake Tahoe Christian Conference Papers*, 1943

In the wake of World War II, the United States emerged as an imperial world power, taking the lead not only in the production of material goods but also in the making of cultural knowledge. While orientalism has its origins in Europe, at this particularly American moment in Western civilization, when America emerged as a formidable presence in international economics and politics, America took the lead in generating a set of images and discourses about the non-West. Given the cordial nature of U.S.–China relations during this period as wartime allies, China held a particular fascination for scholars and policy makers alike, whose unending speculations and queries about its ancient glories, its people, and its future prospects for progress laid the groundwork for Far Eastern Studies programs in universities across America and filled the pages of popular magazines. Of particular interest, for the purposes of this study, are Chinese American cultural ambassadors whose bicultural and bilingual backgrounds afforded them the prestige and position of cultural bridges between the "East" and the "West."

The American image of China dates back to the colonial period and the early trade with the Chinese, but the degree and the level to which orientalist views about China were normalized, domesticated, and popularized in the World War II era is unmatched by any other period in American history.[1] Unique to the American orientalist discourse of this period was the way it tended to measure and define America's others according to carefully calibrated terms of modernity. Modernity at this juncture in history, more than at any other time, was most closely associated with material luxuries and conveniences afforded by the advancement of technology as well as the adoption of beliefs that promoted the progress of civilization. To believe in progress was to believe in the promise of science and the values embedded in American notions of democracy. In short, being American was synonymous with being modern.

The task at hand is not simply to unravel the ideological position of the dominant culture but, crucially, to see how such thinking became part of the self-positioning of American-born Chinese as cultural interpreters between the East and the West. This chapter will examine how the American-born generations, as spearheads of Chinese American culture, forged a new identity for the broader society by posing as cultural bridges between two worlds. In so doing, Chinese Americans were themselves involved in the process of capitalizing on the orientalization of the Chinese for their own benefit. Seeing the longtime hostility against the Chinese suddenly give way to a more auspicious cultural climate, due in large part to China's becoming an ally of the United States and the Japanese bombing of Pearl Harbor, some Chinese Americans joined with non-Chinese American sinologists to help reinvent a view of China and its people as being decidedly modern and American. Banking on their appearance gave them indubitable authenticity as natives, these American-born Chinese spoke with the authority of "native informants."[2] Making strategic use of orientalizing processes, notables like Jade Snow Wong and Pardee Lowe, among others, invented a view of China as at once the seat of ancient and glorious civilization and the promise of a nation reborn into modernity. It would be too simplistic and needlessly judgmental to say that writers like Jade Snow Wong and

Pardee Lowe were merely reinforcing preexisting stereotypes of the Chinese. Rather, their actions challenge the assimilationist perspective that assumes that ethnic subjects typically aspire to blend in with the norms of mainstream America. In fact, they chose to accentuate their cultural differences, albeit selectively, thereby maintaining their integrity as ethnic persons rather than becoming indistinguishable from the rest. While they did enjoy the prestige and social standing that came with being native informants who could adroitly manage the orientalist system, they were actually anthropologists in their own right, generating views about China, its people, and Chinese America that differed in important ways from the prevailing, dominant discourse about the Chinese. First and foremost, they were motivated by the desire to push at the American doors of opportunity for the Chinese, which were only beginning to open in the World War II era. Their views indubitably served to promote the economic and social advancement of Chinese America.

Loyal American Citizens

Unlike the generation of the previous decade, the Chinese American youths of the 1940s could give their political allegiance to America without feeling as though they were compromising the interests of their ancestral land. By the time of the war, Rodney Chow, like many others of the World War II era, had decided against going to China. Chow explained, "By then my feelings had changed, and I was thinking of myself as an American. But the oldtimers used to say to me, 'When you going back to China?' But the answer was, 'How can I go back to some place where I never been from?'"[3]

At the height of friendly relations between China and the United States, Madame Chiang Kai-shek, the wife of the generalissimo of China, addressed the U.S. Senate on 18 February 1943. In her speech, she underscored that both nations shared the same cause and ideals in fighting for freedom.[4] Madame Chiang urged Chinese Americans to join the struggle for American democracy. Margaret Lee of Los Angeles joined the war effort by collecting money for the United China Relief. She recalled walking in the Moon Festival parade with other members of the Mei Wah Girls Club—which did a lot of charity work—and carrying a huge American flag, into which bystanders, including whites, would throw their contributions.[5]

Blessed by Madame Chiang's benediction, "Be good American citizens and you are good Chinese citizens," some 13,499, or 22 percent of all adult American-born Chinese males, enlisted in the U.S. Army.[6] To fight for America was also to fight for China. Eager to prove his patriotism but equally anxious to leave what he called the "miserable life in Chinatown," David Gan tried to enlist in the Navy at the age of seventeen. His poor eyesight, however, held him back. "My eyes were 20/200 and did not meet the enlistment requirements. I had even used my own card . . . [which] had a pin hole on it so I could read the eye chart, but the examiner discovered my ruse. They told me to wait till my eighteenth birthday and the Army would take me." He did wait, and on his eighteenth birthday, he enlisted in the army at the Presidio at Monterey. "I had never felt so happy and proud that I was an American, ready to fight for my country even if it meant that I must give up my life," said Gan.[7] In comparison, the decision to join the war effort was motivated by an entirely different set of circumstances for the Japanese nisei. With their families interned and their citizenship rights jeopardized, many nisei answered the call to fight for American democracy, understandably, with less enthusiasm. The 33,000 nisei soldiers who did serve in the U.S. Armed Forces hoped that by participating in the defense of their country they would prove beyond a doubt that they were indeed loyal citizens of the United States.[8] For Chinese Americans, the invitation to join the war effort opened up new economic opportunities and possibilities for social advancement in America.

To signify their newfound status as loyal Americans, members of the Chinese American Christian Conference officially voted to adopt the term "American-Chinese."[9] While the old term, "American-born Chinese," implied first and foremost an allegiance to their ancestral homeland, the new term, "American-Chinese" or "American of Chinese descent," connoted an undisputed claim to their American status. This term implied that they were privy to the "ideals, government, and institutions of democracy," like any other Americans.[10]

Repeal of Exclusion Acts

As American-Chinese, some felt emboldened to publicly denounce policies and rhetorical practices that denigrated their ancestry. Of primary concern to many Chinese Americans was the repeal of the overtly racist Chinese Exclusion Act, first implemented in 1882, which severely curtailed Chinese immigration and made Chinese ineligible for citizenship. Walter Kong, an American-born Chinese who was educated on the East Coast and had become a prominent businessman in California, observed that the Exclusion Act was particularly onerous to the American-born. Kong argued that due to the lingering racist sentiments contained in the anti-Chinese law, American-born Chinese, who were fully American citizens, were treated as "second-class citizens."[11] To anyone born in America, he complained, the Exclusion Act had become a matter of "deep humiliation" and "a source of untold hardship."[12] The act perpetuated the American public's tendency to see all Chinese Americans, regardless of their American birthplace, as strangers. As a case in point, Kong recounted his own unpleasant encounter with an immigration officer at the Mexican–U.S. border.

Officer: Are you a Chinese?
  Kong: Yes. Chinese American.
Officer: Then, turn back. You cannot go.
  Kong: Why? All these people are going.
Officer: Yes, but you are a Chinese.
  Kong: But I am an American.
Officer: It makes no difference.[13]

On 17 December 1943, the Exclusion Act of 1882 was repealed; in its place, an annual immigration quota of 105 was established for persons of Chinese ancestry. Furthermore, the right to naturalization was conferred upon those who were permanent citizens.[14] The new low immigration quota did not much aid the growth of the Chinese American community. Its significance was more symbolic; it signaled possible end of racist exclusion and the promise of better conditions for Chinese Americans.[15]

The repeal of the exclusion law was the first of a series of other laws designed to improve racial ties between the Chinese and the dominant society. The War Brides Act of 22 July 1947 permitted the entry of eight thousand women, whose presence significantly promoted the growth of families. In the same year, housing restrictions were lifted; for the first time in history, Chinese Americans could buy homes outside of Chinatown ghettos. Finally, the 1872 general law against miscegenation which had been amended in 1903 to include Mongolians, was repealed in 1946.[16]

Opening Doors of Economic Opportunity

On the economic front, increased numbers of Chinese Americans began entering into the mainstream job market. The American-born Chinese who saw firsthand the limited opportunities of an earlier generation could appreciate their somewhat improved lot. Many of their parents were employed in manual labor; more than 60 percent of the Chinese in the labor force were working in restaurants, laundries, and garment factories. Others were chambermaids, janitors, elevator operators, and household servants, while a small percentage were proprietors of groceries, curio and art shops, and drugstores in Chinatown.[17] With the war industry making more jobs available, the Chinese American labor force in the 1940s increased over the previous decade by 11,935.[18] More than 80 percent of these jobs were in industries directly connected with the war effort.[19] Opportunities for engineers, technicians, and scientists in the region's expanding electronics, missiles, and research and development sector opened the gate to Chinese occupational mobility. Those in the professional and technical areas increased from 2.8 percent of the entire Chinese American workforce to 7.1 percent.[20] In a year's time, Chinese workers in clerical and professional positions increased to about 38 percent of the Chinese workforce.[21] At the same time, there was a reduction of those in manual labor from 63.7 percent in 1940 to 54.5 percent a decade later.[22] The growth was most significant in the area of white-collar occupations. Those working in the clerical and sales jobs, which included many in the younger native-born generation, rose from 4,172 in 1940 to 7,722 in 1950.[23] Those with a college education sometimes held jobs as engineers, technicians, and scientists in the electronics and missile research and development.[24]

The Liberal Racial Logic of the World War II Era

These improvements within Chinese America were made possible in part by the generally more liberal racial climate. A pivotal change in the racial thinking of America during World War II helped to soften the harshly negative view of the Chinese rooted in the general xenophobic atmosphere of nineteenth-century America. This strain of racial discourse came to be replaced by a more enlightened one, intended to contradict the former thinking that human beings could be divided into distinct races on the basis of ostensible phenotypic characteristics. Confronted with the horrifying consequences of the eugenics movement rooted in Nazi racial ideology, social pundits and the scientific community banded together, speaking out vehemently against the racist logic that made judgments about human character, intelligence, and culture based on such arbitrary factors as the color of one's skin and hair or the shape of one's nose and eyes. Racism was perceived as being akin to fascism. In this politically charged atmosphere, Ruth Benedict, in her book *Race: Science and Politics* (1940), equated the fight against racism with "making democracy work."[25] Equally concerned with the contradictions between the ideal of democracy on the one hand, and the practical problem of racism on the other, Gunnar Myrdal published what has become a classic treatise on the racial problem at the heart of American identity: *The American Dilemma: The Negro Problem and Modern Democracy* (1944). In it he described the "moral dilemma of the American" as

> the ever-raging conflict between, on the one hand, the valuations preserved on the general plane which we shall call the "American Creed," where the American thinks, talks, and acts under the influence of high national and Christian precepts, and, on the other hand, the valuations on specific planes of individual and group living, where personal and local interests; economic, social, and sexual jealousies . . . dominate his outlook.[26]

From a purely biological standpoint, Gunnar Dahlberg in his *Race, Reason, and Rubbish: An Examination of the Biological Credentials of the Nazi Creed* (1943) contended that the term "race" could not be justifiably applied to human beings since "it has been known that different types of human beings in different parts of the world can interbreed."[27] From his standpoint as a physical anthropologist, Ashley Montagu agreed that while there were "distinctive populations" of the human species, "distinct races" were an impossibility, given how "all human beings are so much mixed with regard to origin." He pointed to the difficulty of drawing up "more than a few hard and fast distinctions between even the most extreme types."[28]

Montagu's book *Man's Most Dangerous Myth: The Fallacy of Race* (1942), a clear indictment of the classical anthropological conception of "race," argued that it was "artificial" in the sense that it was socially constructed; that it did not "correspond with the facts" of science; and that it led to "confusion and the perpetuation of error." For these reasons, the author advocated that the term "race" "be dropped altogether from the vocabulary" (70). To bolster his cause, he advocated interracial unions not only because they blurred the lines of racial boundaries but also for the benefit of a stronger and better human race:

> Just as the fertilizing effects of the contact and mixing of cultures lead to the growth and development of the older forms of culture and the creation of new ones within it, so, too, does the interbreeding of different ethnic groups lead to the growth and development of the physical stock of mankind. It is through the agency of interbreeding that nature, in the form of man's genetic system, shows its creative power. (187).

Actually, Montagu's vision of a multicultural society that cherished rather than stigmatized cultural difference and human variation promoted a version of Americanization more nuanced than the "melting pot" thesis. Cautioning against "cultural differences" becoming "swallowed up and annihilated too soon," he encouraged instead the "blending of what is best" from many different cultures combined with an intact preservation of "the unique virtues of culture" (251). He noted that cultural differences were sorely obliterated "even before the dominant culture has grasped their meaning" (251). In theory, Montagu's model of cross-cultural interchange appears to be a mutually giving and receiving, a two-way process; in reality, he leaves intact the framework that favors America's mainstream culture and renders cultural difference as a set of tributaries merely contributing toward the mainstream. The American-born Chinese who saw themselves as the cultural bridge understood and capitalized on the precise nature of such liberal racial logic.

The Friendly versus Enemy Aliens

Indeed, for Chinese Americans, race no longer posed itself as an obstacle denying them access and entry into public places. Ruth Wong, who resided in San Francisco during the war, recounted that being Chinese meant the difference between being served or not being served in a restaurant. Whenever she stepped outside of her home, Wong would wear a button that stated in no uncertain terms, "I am Chinese." Chinese Americans who did this avoided needless harassment from whites. Wong recalled a time when she forgot to wear her button: At a café in San Francisco, she waited indefinitely to be served until she produced her ID. "They didn't serve me because they thought I was Japanese. The Japanese were really hated by the Caucasian people. Sometimes I would stand there waiting and waiting to be served and I would ask why I'm not being served. They would say, 'Are you Japanese?' and when I said, 'No,' they would apologize for not serving me sooner."[29]

During the war era, Chinese and the Japanese were pitted against each other; the Chinese were depicted as the friendly, assimilable race, and the Japanese as enemy aliens. The growing image of Japan as a bellicose nation harboring imperialist designs for China, if not for all of Asia, further encouraged the thinking that if the Japanese were the enemy aliens, then the Chinese were an assimilable, friendly race. The results of a Gallup Poll conducted in 1942 reflected the image of the Chinese versus the Japanese in the minds of the American public. The Japanese were thought to be "sly, treacherous, war-like, and cruel," whereas the Chinese were "honest, hard-working, and religious."[30] The negative image of the Japanese actually went back to a period before the war, when it became obvious to the American public that Japan posed a major threat to China and much of Asia. When the Japanese attacked the Chinese forces at Marco Polo Bridge, southwest of Beijing, on 7 July 1936, immense public sympathy for the Chinese was aroused. Japan's invasion of China posed not only a military but also an economic threat, as America's foreign policy makers feared that a defeated China would also mean losing China as America's market. In 1936, 25 percent of China's total imports had come from the United States. By May of 1939, 74 percent of Americans expressed that they supported China in the Sino-Japanese War. Anti-Japanese feelings came to a head when Japan bombed Pearl Harbor on 7 December 1941.[31] As the Japanese became the clear enemy in the eyes of America, the Chinese rose in its estimation as kindly and assimilable.

A survey of popular journals showcased articles such as "How to Tell the Japs from the Chinese" or, more explicitly, "How to Tell Your Friends from the Japs," which were meant to serve as guides to aid the American public in making the fine distinctions.[32] Even while "an anthropologist, with calipers and plenty of time to measure heads, noses, shoulders, hips," wrote the writer of *Time*, could admittedly sometimes be "stumped," the experts could still suggest "a few rules of thumb." The Chinese were said to have a "parchment yellow complexion," while the Japanese had "an earthy yellow complexion"; the Chinese were tall and fat, whereas the Japanese were short and skinny. In reading their faces, the public could see that the "Chinese expression is likely to be more placid, kindly, [and] open," while "the Japanese is more positive, dogmatic, [and] arrogant." Another point of distinction, if all else failed, was the "walk"; the Japanese "walk stiffly erect and hard-heeled," whereas the Chinese walked with "a more relaxed, easy gait" like "a shuffle." Alex Harlicka, a resident anthropologist at the Smithsonian Institution, was of the opinion that identification using physical points of distinction had only a 30 percent chance of producing correct identification. A more reliable judgment, he claimed, could be made with the study of "manners" and "psychological expressions." To the growing list of distinctions, Harlicka explained that the Japanese have "a clever, smarter expression—the reflection of their materialistic and commercial interests"—

whereas the Chinese had faces that the anthropologists found "kind, friendly and interesting."[33]

Chinese on the Brink of Modernity

Lin Yutang, a premier sinologist of this period, seized upon the favorable climate toward the Chinese by writing numerous scholarly and popularized texts in order to capture the imagination and the sympathy of the mainstream audience. Yutang, a leading figure among China's emerging scholars, was born and raised in China but was educated in the West. He was therefore optimally situated to become the expert insider, able to translate things Chinese to the Western audience. No work, excepting perhaps Pearl S. Buck's *The Good Earth*, was more influential in shaping the views of the Chinese than his *My Country, My People* (1935). His work merits a close examination, not only because it was influential but also because his thinking and writing paved the way for American-born China experts like Jade Snow Wong and Pardee Lowe to position themselves similarly as cultural bridges between the East and the West. While there were no formal ties established between this Chinese émigré and Chinese American China experts, they found themselves nonetheless involved in a similar discourse.

Lin Yutang was masterful in the art of persuasion. *My Country, My People* neither offended Western readers nor required them to change what they already thought they knew about China and its people. In a lighthearted, bantering spirit, he confirmed the stereotype that the Chinese were in fact ill equipped to take on modernization. Still, he argued, with a strong commitment and willful attention given to the task at hand, the Chinese people would indeed be fully capable of modernizing.

Yutang described China's fate as hanging in the balance between tradition and rebirth.[34] Echoing the advice of American political pundits and sinologists, Lin Yutang advocated modernization, which he delineated as "an inexorable process brought about by the spread of newspapers and radios and a thousand other contacts with the West."[35] Yutang painted a picture of the Chinese people as being

quintessentially "mellow."[36] Being inherently "passive" and "calm"
to a fault, they were less disposed to "youthful enthusiasm for progress
and reform" (44). While these qualities were conducive to a civilization "built for strength and endurance," they were said to be less
useful for "progress and conquest" (44). Lin Yutang portrayed the
Chinese as tragicomic figures, not unintelligent, whose inherent disposition made them difficult to change: "At its worst, this old rogu-
ery, which is the highest product of Chinese intelligence, works
against idealism and action. It shatters all desire for reform, laughs at
the futility of idealism and action. It has a strange way of reducing all
human activities to the level of the alimentary canal and other simple
biological needs" (53).

The problem lay in the Chinese mind, which was said to be essentially "feminine," to the extent that it was "full of common sense,"
"synthetic and concrete," and devoid of "abstract" thinking (80). Similarly, as compared to the "masculine" English language, Chinese was
feminine in form, syntax, and vocabulary, which were highly simplistic (81). Along similar lines, the Chinese were said to be incapable of logical thought, as evidenced by their lack of interest in
developing a science of grammar, mathematics, and astronomy. With
little penchant for play and experimentation, they had not made any
great discoveries or invented new methods in science (86). Yutang
concluded that if the Chinese worked against their natural proclivi-
ties, they also could achieve modernization.[37]

Lin Yutang's China reverberated in the minds of many Americans. As a Chinese scholar born and raised in China, and educated in
both countries, he was amply qualified, in the eyes of white America,
to be the spokesperson for the Chinese. His writings, which appeared
in popular journals like *Reader's Digest, Colliers, Harper's Magazine, Asia,* and *Atlantic,* were influential in shaping the public's ideas
about the Chinese. Although his views on the Chinese were often
surprising, humorous, and nonconventional, they left intact the
orientalist framework that essentialized the Chinese character as
being passive and unimaginative. His China was in every way opposite to America. If China was backward, then America and the West
as a whole were progressive; if China was feminine, then the West

was masculine. By making the West his point of reference, Lin Yutang validated the Eurocentric assumption that the West was normative. Nor did he challenge the thinking endemic to modernism that assumed that it was possible to measure progress through time in a linear progression. Caught up in wartime optimism, he, like many others, saw the West, in particular the United States of America, as the best of all possible worlds, against which all other nations' progress was to be measured.

Taking its cue from Yutang and others, the popular printed media similarly portrayed the Chinese as reluctant converts to modernity. Rufus Suter, a writer for *Scientific American*, wrote that the future success of China depended on the extent to which it could become modernized. In order to join the "world powers," China, though once a "refined civilization," had to catch up with the West, which had given birth to modern science and launched the age of reason.[38] "For centuries the culture of this so-called 'backward' nation was the equal of, and in some respects superior to, that of western nations."[39] Until the eighteenth century, China had been in a "state of animation," but it had lagged seriously behind during the birth of modern science in the West.[40] Chinese "backwardness" was thought by some to be a direct result of the Chinese mind. "Indeed their discoveries and inventions were well nigh numberless," stated Suter, "but Chinese natural knowledge always remained piecemeal," for the Chinese lacked the capacity to turn them into "an organized whole."[41] Hence it was unlikely that the Chinese would make any discoveries that would permit a "farsighted, effective control of nature on a vast scale."[42] Lester Walker in *Harper's Magazine* confirmed that, in short, "precision, systems, the techniques of scientific logic" were antithetical to the "Chinese thought pattern."[43] He posited that an examination of the Chinese language mirrored this essentially backward nature of the Chinese. "China is shackled by its own written language," Walker wrote, since Chinese, consisting of "highly stylized pictures," is not only inefficient but incapable also of rendering expressions "in modern concepts."[44]

In spite of the obstacles presumably posed by the Chinese character, a minority generally sympathetic to the Chinese came to believe that China was slowly but surely becoming modernized. Amanda Boyden, a reporter from *National Geographic* magazine, praised the Chinese for showing themselves to be "remarkably adaptable in adjusting themselves to contact with English-speaking nations," the proof of which lay in their adoption of "automobiles, foreign clothes, Jazz, and golf."[45] Sometimes their imitation of things Western were said to be better than the originals. In Shanghai, the tailors were said to do even a better job than Western ones in making "foreign suits."[46] Another writer pointed to how the modern city of Peiping had broken with a four-thousand-year tradition by adopting the Western calendar in lieu of the lunar one. Though once a stronghold of conservatism in the North, Peiping announced that it would celebrate the new year with the modern world, on the first of January.[47] There were examples, moreover, of some individuals like a Mr. Chu whom the author, Mildred Hand, described as a "passionate modernist" who had bravely broken with the ancient practice of "ancestor worship."[48]

Even as some applauded China's modernizing efforts, they bemoaned the passing of certain antiquarian aspects of old China. In what the anthropologist Renate Rosaldo called "imperialist nostalgia," the cultural reportage of this era sentimentalized the passing of memorable personages, who, however anachronistic, were nonetheless virtuous and noble heroes holding on to a way of life out of synch with the modernist impulse current in the rest of the world.[49] Romanticizing the Chinese character, these writers offered sentimentalized portraits of Chinese people who epitomized nobility, gentleness, and patience, traits long recognized as being quintessentially Chinese. An apt metaphor of times gone by, the eunuchs of Peiping, who once served in the Manchu court, were heralded by James Burke as "the last relic" of old China.[50] Though once a formidable presence in the Manchu empire, numbering over three thousand, the handful of remaining eunuchs had grown into old, feeble creatures who would "gladly pose for a small fee," no longer able to grow "rich on graft" as they had done in bygone days.[51] Much of the discussion, however, centered around the lives of everyday people who exuded what many reporters called a "timeless" quality, as compared to the quick and impatient temperament of modern people. Dorothy Graham, a writer for *Catholic World,* wrote, "Even in transition, China will be timeless," since the Chinese "have a contempt for chaos."[52] She wrote that through three thousand years of war, floods, and famine, the Chinese people had been able "to attain an essential calm within themselves."[53] In that way, the Chinese, as opposed to the Westerner, was predictable and unchanging. Corroborating this view, Samuel Blythe wrote about a certain Chinese cook who was an "ageless oriental," confirming that "nobody who is white knows how old a Chinese is."[54] An "exemplary servant" all his life, the nameless cook was praised for his "loyalty, thrift, industry, and devoted service."[55] In a piece called "The Most Unforgettable Character I've Ever Met," the writer Pearl S. Buck wrote about Madame Hsiung, an elderly upper-class woman. Practiced in the Confucian style of the traditional Chinese family, Madame Hsiung, for whom "her family was of utmost importance," managed her clan with a tidy intelligence. "Strong, cunning, powerful, and beautiful," Madame Hsiung, according to Buck, was "every bit a woman."[56] Thomas Handforth, an artist, was equally an admirer of the Chinese; he went from town to town, gathering portraits and stories. He told a story of an orphan girl named Mei Li who impressed him with her "wit, beauty, charm, and daring."[57] In the artist's eyes, Mei Li's candor and innocence were rare indeed.

The discourse about the Chinese from these Western sinologists tended to emphasize the incompatibility of Eastern thinking and character with Western notions of progress. In the classic assimilationist formulation, one could not remain genuinely Chinese and also be modern. Indeed, one had to give up the Chinese character in order to become modern. In contrast to this polarized thinking, American-born Chinese like Jade Snow Wong and Pardee Lowe, representing a sentiment popular among their cohort, posited that one could be Chinese and still be modern. By taking the best of both East and West, Chinese Americans were said to occupy both worlds at the same time. They turned upside down the prototypical notion of the second generation as the troubled and marginal into a positive, more enabling image of the cultural ambassador.

The Bridge between the East and the West

"We occupy a most unique position," William Hoy wrote for the Lake Tahoe Conference papers, "standing betwixt the cultures and traditions of our forefathers and that of the land of our birth."[58] In this liminal space, some members of the second generation positioned themselves strategically to serve as ambassadors to both their parents and the dominant culture. The essayist stated that the role of the Chinese American second generation was to "explain the American ways" to their parents and to "interpret the Chinese culture and civilization" to white America.[59] In so doing, they might fulfill a "manifest duty" to "penetrate beyond superficial differences and bring forth the best elements of these two different streams of civilization."[60] American-born Chinese, the essayist continued, could contribute to the Chinese community a "technological and scientific" knowledge gained by studying Western civilization. To the West, whose thinking was "essentially experimental," they might teach Chinese philosophy, which was said to be much more "humanistic." Instead of being "worried with how to earn a living," he advised that they do "maximum service to society" as "spearheads of culture." "Bridging cultures" became the philosophical metaphor describing the marriage of "occidental and oriental" cultures.[61] Incidentally and ironically, only a decade earlier, the nisei also had fashioned themselves as cultural "intermediaries," interpreting the East to the West and the West to the East. Serving as the "bridge" (*kakehashi*), they too had hoped that better cultural understanding would lead to improved relations with the dominant society.[62]

Pardee Lowe

Charged with a similar enthusiasm and purpose, Pardee Lowe wrote a memoir, *Father and Glorious Descendant* (1943). He revisits a familiar trope in Asian American literature equating Asia with traditionalism and America with modernity. In spite of all the ways that the two cultures differ from one another, Pardee asserts, what is held in common is patriarchy. In *Father and Glorious Descendant*, patriarchy becomes coded as a sign describing modernity that is couched within an explicitly masculinist construction invoking the characteristics, rites, and manners of a model patriarch, embodied in the person of his father and Pardee himself.

"I sometimes suspect that my father's life is a fraud," begins Pardee Lowe, casting doubt over the legitimacy of his father's claim that he was born in America. Given the benefits of citizenship, many Chinese immigrants claimed American-born status, taking advantage of the 1906 San Francisco earthquake, which destroyed many municipal records. The investigation of his father's identity becomes the focal point of his memoir. Conflicting stories about his origins notwithstanding, Pardee is undiminished in his admiration of his father, who is at once a Chinese traditional and a modern. His father's "bushy mustache," his queueless head without a bowler hat, and his well-tailored suit make him stand apart from the average Chinaman with "vermillion braids."[63] It was his "growing sense of modernism" in the first place that made him resolve to have a Western-style marriage, which, of course, included going queueless (12). It was his "modern sensibility" that guided him in choosing American names for his children (16). Perhaps the greatest proof of his modernist approach to life, however, is evidenced in his capacity as a model father and leader within his community. As a model civic leader, he is often called upon to adjudicate disputes among extended family and clan members and to resolve tong wars. His ability as a conciliator is matched by his manly prowess, demonstrated by his capacity to chase down an armed bandit. "Imbued with the republican principle" (16), "wise and intelligent," and capable of "winning the respect of barbarians," (76), his father possessed all the characteristics of a commanding patriarch, referred to by some as "the duke" (135). Though his father's nativity still remains dubious by the end of the memoir, the legality of his father's American citizenship is rendered moot as Lowe amply establishes that his father indeed has earned his right to be an American.

There is an explicitly materialist dimension to Lowe's father's modernity. Ever dutiful and responsive to the material needs of his kin, the patriarch provides handsomely for his family and other relations. Buying a house in East Belleville, a traditionally white neighborhood, and sending his children to nonsegregated schools, are evidence of his penchant for modernity. The defining touch, making him a bona fide modern, comes with his purchase of the "polychromic bathtub" in his newly built three-story apartment house (82). At a time when, according to the 1940 census, 31 percent of the 34 million dwelling units in the United States still lacked running water; 32 percent used an outside toilet; and 39 percent did not have a bathtub or a shower— even one shared with other tenants—the shiny new bathtub takes on an added significance.[64] Pardee Lowe here produces an explicitly materialist expression of modernity and crucially points to the possibility of a compatibility between maintaining Chinese cultural identity and being a successful American.

To be modern, according to Lowe, one not only has to embrace a certain worldview rooted in American democracy and individualism; one also has to demonstrate it outwardly. That is, modernity for Lowe has as much to do with what he wears, where and how he lives, and what he does for a living as with what he thinks. These marks of upward class mobility have set his father apart from the rest of the Chinese who live in Chinatown, and have afforded him the distinction of being modern. Pardee Lowe's construction of the modern Chinese American stands in direct contrast to the prevailing image of the Chinese rooted in nineteenth-century stereotype, which portrays the Chinese as occupying the lowest rung on the socioeconomic ladder. He explains that he has grown tired of the way the Chinese are associated with "slavery, concubinage, prostitution, the opium vice, the disease of leprosy—and the lowest standard of living known" (35). Half a century after the height of the Working Party's campaign to scapegoat the Chinese as the antithesis of the American way of life, Lowe can still recite the odious slogan "To an American death is preferable to a life on a par with the Chinaman!" (35).

Challenging the familiar tension between cultural integrity and economic success that is said to exist in ethnic and immigrant minorities, Lowe shows that both tendencies can be satisfied in the person of his father. In spite of his modernist tendencies, his father is depicted as a Chinese traditionalist, although he sometimes rebels against the strictures of his tradition. Were it not for the women in his life, however, Lowe's father would not be able to maintain or transfer the riches of Chinese tradition onto his progeny. Lowe's depiction of women further corroborates his masculinist construction of modernity. Women are depicted as priestesses of Chinese rites and ceremonies. In this way, the women become the gatekeepers of Chinese culture. Lowe describes his mother as a complete outsider to the Western world, who, with her "realistic Chinese soul," exclaims, "My, my, what queer people the Americans are!" (127). After his mother's passing, his Elder Paternal Aunt Jo replaces her as the official priestess in family gatherings. Lowe and his father come to the conclusion that "women are always superstitious." When it comes to superstitious beliefs, his father tells Lowe, men and women are simply different. "If it makes your Mother and Aunt Jo happy, who are we to object? We are men, and worshipping is not our affair. Let them pray for good fortune and we will try to make it" (71). As Lowe comes of age and becomes a father himself, he attains greater appreciation for the way that women preserve and pass down the ancient rites and traditions that afford them the luxury of being Chinese. The Chinese women become the guardians of their ethnic identity as Chinese Americans.

When he returns from his forays in American education at Harvard and becomes a father himself, he becomes far less critical and a willing participant in these ceremonies. Through the writing of his autobiographical memoir, Pardee also becomes a translator and purveyor of Chinese rites to his American readership and his American-born son. As the ethnic ethnographer, he provides the purported insider's insight into such traditions as the ancient medicinal cures like the wildcat soup; the traditional marriage rite; and the longevity gown ceremony. In this way, he becomes the cultural ambassador bridging the gap between the polarities represented by Chinese women (who symbolize Chinese tradition and culture) and his Western audience. As the translator of things Chinese, he shows a brand of Chinese culture that is sanitized and simplified so as not to pose any threat to his Western audience. In describing his stepmother's practice of ancestral worship, he is careful to talk about it in terms his audience will understand and appreciate. Observing his stepmother,

"her hands upraised to the emerald-blue of the morning skies, clasping a sheaf of fragrant incense," Lowe, who was once "aggressively intolerant of her strange religious ways," becomes a convert to her "humility and sincerity"—characteristics said to be no different from those of the Puritan Fathers. However "barbaric it might have appeared in form and details to alien eyes," his stepmother's worship comes to symbolize for Lowe "the deeply religious heart whose prayers are grounded in universal humanity" (308).

Lowe's story ends with a festive family gathering of three generations who have come to pay respects to his aged father in the longevity feast.

> I gazed once more on that scene of lively color and noise, Father's Longevity Feast. I wanted to fix it forever in my memory so that someday when Tsu-I grew to manhood, I could tell him the complete story of his Grandfather's Great Birthday. I would explain to him why the Longevity Party was such a success, and why even in the Western World, even in Chinatown, the old traditions prevailed. (321–322)

In this scene, he brings home the point that Chinese traditionalism can live side by side with Western modernism. Appropriately, at the end of the book, Lowe returns to pay homage to the patriarch who is depicted throughout as the exemplary embodiment of the best of the East and the West.

Through the writing of *Father and Glorious Descendant*, Lowe established his role as a cultural interpreter, translating Chinese ways to his American audience. In addition to his memoir, Lowe frequently wrote about life in Chinatown in popular and academic journals like *Asia* and *The Yale Review*. Posing as the insider anthropologist, he talked selectively about a Chinatown that was becoming progressively modern in appearance while still maintaining its customs and traditions. In a piece called "The Good Life in Chinatown: Further Adventures of a Chinese Husband and His American Wife Among His Own People" (1937), he achieved, through distancing, an intimate and yet "objective" interpretation of "the social life of San Francisco's Chinatown." He described his "investigation," modeled after the school of anthropology based in a scientific method of reasoning and fieldwork, as being the result of meticulous observations of his people's activities and behavior in settings like Chinese celebrations, family feasts, marriages, funerals, and birthings. The fact that he was married to a white woman helped to facilitate his role as the ethnic ethnographer, since he found in his American wife a willing outsider who lived safely in a community that had once been thought to be a menace to the well-being and integrity of white women. A biographer and amateur anthropologist, Lowe wrote in both popular and academic media about the social and cultural life of the Chinese in America as a people at once traditionally Chinese and American modern.[65]

Jade Snow Wong

Echoing a sentiment similar to that of Pardee Lowe, Jade Snow Wong stated that "creating better understanding between Americans and the Chinese" was "the guiding theme" of her life and her writings.[66] Jade Snow Wong also wrote an autobiographical memoir called *Fifth Chinese Daughter* (1945), which provides an open window onto the study of the cultural bridge as an operative framework in the invention of Chinese American identity and culture in the 1940s. In the preface to her memoir, Wong explained her role as a cultural bridge whose function was to "explain the Chinese culture to the Americans."[67]

The narrative in *Fifth Chinese Daughter* follows the trajectory of a Chinese American daughter whose life circumstances and experiences lead her to become a cultural bridge. Unlike Lowe, whose place in his family as the honored first-born son affords certain inalienable privileges and rights, Jade Snow Wong must fight to prove her worth in her family by making a name for herself in the broader society. Her role as the cultural interpreter is therefore as much an effort to gain esteem among her own people as it is to create a niche for herself in the larger society.

The story begins with the recounting of an early childhood episode that illustrates the painful reality of her "two-ness." It is difficult to grow up in a society in which the idea of the tragic mulatto or the related notion of the marginal man, amply evident in the popular American psyche and its literature, works to normalize and authenticate the unhyphenated identity. Wong wonders how she is to live with biculturalism. Written in the third person, the book relates the "specific" nature of difference between the American and the Chinese way. Wong describes the confusion and the discomfort that results when she compares the ways of her parents with those of Miss Mullohand:

> It was a very strange feeling to be held up to a grown-up foreign lady's bosom. She could not remember when Mama had held her to give comfort. . . . There in Miss Mullohand's arms, with undefined confusion in her mind, she suddenly remembered the time when she and Jade Precious Stone had awakened from Sunday afternoon naps to find the whole store dark and deserted, and the front door locked. But Mama and Daddy had not caught them up in their arms in comfort, Jade Snow remembered at first, finding it wonderful comfort to be embraced by Miss Mullohand. But suddenly the comfort changed to embarrassment. What was one supposed to do now in response? The embarrassment turned to panic. . . . She was conscious that "foreign" American ways were not only generally and vaguely different from their Chinese ways, but that they were specifically different, and that specific difference would involve a choice of action. Jade Snow had begun to compare American ways with those of her mother and father and the comparison made her uncomfortable. (20–21)

That she favors American ways over the Chinese ways of her parents at an early age is not surprising, since she is a product of her American schooling, which emphasizes the normative construction of identity that favors American individualism and disparages authoritarian tradition. For Jade Snow, who has had to battle against Chinese patriarchy from a young age, American individualism is particularly attractive. Being born a Chinese female places her in a clear disadvantage within her family, since she has to constantly prove herself as capable as her brothers in making a name for herself and gaining the respect of her family. She learns at a relatively young age that her sex places her in a subordinate position; this is a defining moment in the formation of her identity. That her parents should name her newly arrived sibling "Forgiveness from Heaven" born fifteen years after the birth of "Blessing from Heaven," her older brother, causes her to feel "uncomfortable"; she wonders whether, as girls, her "dear baby sister Precious Stone" and she herself are somehow "less significant" than the boys in her family (27). Given this penchant toward individualized identity and the disparagement of women's worth in Chinese patriarchy, Wong rebels against the ways of her seemingly authoritarian parents, whose Chinese values clash with her own American ones. Wong describes her early adult years as continually plagued by "the pull from both cultures," which leaves her dizzy in a whirlwind of confused emotions (132). In this period of clashing cultures, Wong adopts the prevailing view that the West is liberating, whereas the East is oppressive. In reading the first half of the autobiography, the reader wonders how Jade Snow will bridge these seemingly irreconcilable cultures.

It is only when she leaves home and goes away to Mills College that Jade Snow comes to have a new appreciation and renewed interest in Chinese culture. In this second phase of her identity formation, she comes to see her biculturalism not as a problem but as an asset that promises to open up new career options in mainstream America. At Mills College, she quickly realizes the benefits of making Chinese culture the focus of her studies. She explains that her "grades were consistently higher when she wrote about Chinatown and the people she had known all her life" (132). Seeing how the educated elite are "genuinely curious to learn about her culture," Wong begins to take courses on Chinese art history, language, and pottery so as to become more knowledgeable (161). With her newly gained knowledge about China, Wong becomes a valuable storehouse of generalized information about China and its language, customs, history, the culinary arts, pottery, painting, and literature rooted in ancient China. Her self-fashioned role as a cultural interpreter, then, is arguably a calculated response to the opportunity for making a living in mainstream America, rather than one motivated simply by a desire to assimilate. She capitalizes on mainstream curiosity. Having embraced her newfound identity and mission as cultural interpreter, no longer is the author torn between two cultures; rather, she espouses the clear benefits of maintaining "a balance between old ways and the new ways" (96). In order to strike a more harmonious balance between the two systems, Wong states, she first has had to come to a deeper "understanding of the old ways" of her parents (96). Emerging as the cultural bridge, she sheds the torment of her former identity crisis and negotiates a bicultural identity that is spun out of what she calls the best of the East and the West, echoing the liberal, cultural pluralist logic of the times.

Unlike Pardee Lowe, who frequently poses as the observer as opposed to the participant, Jade Snow Wong is more often than not herself a performer in the Chinese rituals and other cultural practices about which she provides a carefully guided commentary. That is, she turns herself into an ethnographic spectacle by putting herself on public display and performing as the Chinese potter or the cook before her admiring white audience. Wong describes her performance as the Chinese cook when she cooks a Chinese meal for a group of musicians gathered at the Dean's house at Mills College: "That was a wonderful evening. . . . For the first time, Jade Snow felt an important participant in the role of hostess. Because of everyone's interest in the kitchen preparations, she soon lost her shyness in the presence of celebrities and acted naturally. There was no talk about music, only about Chinese food" (173). She describes how she feels and acts "naturally" in this setting and remains silent about any feelings of being essentialized as the Chinese cook. Perhaps the fact that she is appreciated compensates for any misgivings she may have about her role. That is, this culinary scene makes perfect sense when juxtaposed with the one that she remembers as a "torturous nightmare" when she has to cook an "American dinner" with a meringue pie for the Simpsons, who little appreciate or even recognize that such a thing as Chinese cooking exists.

Occasions like these, when she is able to proudly display her Chinese cultural heritage, strengthen her resolve to serve as the cultural bridge between two cultures. Making adroit use of talents that come to her naturally, Wong chooses a career that becomes both her mission and her profession. She becomes a shopkeeper, setting up a pottery shop crucially placed at the outskirts of Chinatown. By putting herself on display, throwing her pots in the storefront, she draws in curious passersby. Her pottery, decorated in distinctively Chinese colors, sells well to an audience with a taste for things Chinese.

The story of Jade Snow Wong, exemplifying the narrative of the American dream, begins with immigrant hardships and ends with American-style success. And yet her thinking differs from the Americanization thesis; she maintains that one can be thoroughly Chinese and still be American modern—that is, she does not need to shed her ethnic heritage to become a bona fide American. Arguing essentially that the modern-day Chinese America is also the repository of China's ancient glories, Wong invokes the preexisting image of primitive China as being highly advanced and civilized. At a time when Chinese Americans were beginning to be seen in a more favorable light, Wong helped to promote and shape the thinking that the Chinese in America not only could catch up with the rest of America; they could make invaluable cultural contributions to mainstream America.

Chinese American Moderns

Dancing in step with the likes of Ginger Rogers and Fred Astaire, some Chinese American entertainers of this time showed a hitherto unknown jazzier, modern side of Chinese America. An interesting if anomalous phenomenon in the World War II era was the emergence of Chinese American nightclubs and bars in metropolitan areas like San Francisco. The Chinese Village, Chinese Pagoda, Jade Palace, Ricksha, Twin Dragons, Chinese Sky Room, Club Shanghai, Dragon's Lair, Kubla Khan, and Lion's Den were some of the nightclubs frequented by both Chinese and white clientele.[68] On 363 Sutter Street stood Forbidden City, the oldest and the most famous of these, owned by Charlie Low. With an impressive all-Chinese floor show and its own band, the nightclub opened in the winter of 1938 and quickly rose in fame and notoriety as one of the hottest spots in

San Francisco. "I wanted to present the modern version of the Chinese girl," explained Charlie Low, "not the old fashioned way, all bundled up with four or five pairs of trousers. . . . Chinese have limbs just as pretty as anyone else."[69]

Forbidden City, geographically located on the border of Chinatown, occupied a culturally liminal space as well, in the way it came to represent the various multifaceted, ambiguous, and tenuous links and relations between the Chinese in America and the larger society at a time when Chinese Americans had begun to have greater visibility in the eyes of the American public.

Unlike Jade Snow Wong and Pardee Lowe, who, while showing themselves to be modern in their sensibilities and style, nonetheless adhered faithfully to cultural forms and practices purportedly belonging to traditional China, these Western-style entertainers did not identify at all with traditional Chinese artistic and cultural forms. Irreverent and rebellious, this segment of the American-born population took a different path. Defying parental advice to become good mothers, merchants, or laundrymen, some of these rebels left their families and pursued dreams of becoming singers and dancers. Jadin Wong ended up in Hollywood, after escaping from her bedroom window one night. Though nearly starving and penniless, she danced, auditioned successfully for some small parts, and found Hollywood overall to be a dazzling place in a way that Stockton, California, her "very square" hometown, never was. "When I started to dance, people thought our family went to the dogs," recalled Wong. Her story typified the lives of many Chinese American aspiring talents who left the narrow confines of what was expected of "decent" Chinese American people in pursuit of extravagant dreams.[70]

Many older Chinese Americans reprimanded the young for failing to measure up to their notion of what constituted good and decent Chinese. "Dancing just was not a part of Chinese culture," explained Mary Mammon, a dancer at Forbidden City.[71] Realizing that his father would never come to accept his career of choice, Paul Wing also decided to leave his home in Stanford, California. His father, confronted with a son who would rather spend his time dancing with a kitchen chair than do his homework, turned to his wife and dejectedly exclaimed, "You know your number one son, something gone wrong somewhere."[72] Jadin added, "Chinese people in San Francisco were ready to spit in our faces because we were nightclub performers."[73] The strong prejudice against performers was actually rooted in the Confucian tradition, which ranked the social status of entertainers on par with prostitutes, thieves, and vagrants. Had these performers grown up in Chinatown proper, they might not have ventured to go into show business. But having grown up in more remote areas—far enough away from the disapproving gaze of Chinatown old-timers—many did not think twice about pursuing their love for the stage.

If some members of the Chinese community derided these seemingly all-too-Americanized youngsters, a largely white clientele enthusiastically applauded them. The major selling point for a successful place like Forbidden City was its all-Chinese floor show. Speculating on why it was so popular, Mary Mammon answered, "We were a novelty."[74] In other words, the white clientele was drawn to the anomaly of "orientals" imitating Western song and dance. Surmising that the Chinese American performers were Chinese nationals, some marveled that they could even sing in English. Others asked if they could touch them, not ever having seen real Chinese before.[75]

Confronted with the highly exotic image of the oriental, many responded by strategically invoking their ethnicity to sell their act. Tony Wing, who described himself as a "chop-suey"—part Chinese, Portuguese, and Puerto Rican—changed his name to an obviously Chinese-sounding one.[76] Jadin Wong learned to wear her hair long in the back with Chinadoll bangs in the front and to dress herself in Chinese chingsom dresses with substantial slits to show her legs.[77] Noel Toy performed her famous nude act known as the "Bubble Dance," knowing how many would come to satisfy their curiosity about the purported malformation of Asian female genitalia. "Oh sure, didn't you know," she'd reply jokingly to the racist and lurid questions put to her about Asian female parts, "it's just like eating corn on the cob."[78]

Being in the entertainment business sometimes required the female entertainers to reinforce the existing image of the Chinadoll, made famous in Hollywood by Anna Mae Wong. Mary Mammon described how the Chinese American female entertainers fit the stereotype operative at the time. "In this particular case, being small was a good thing. They thought we were cute and so dainty. . . . In other words, we were little Chinadolls."[79] Jadin Wong, who also filled this role, stated that she had no qualms about what she did, reasoning thus: "You'd do anything to get noticed. If you say, no, you're lying."[80] Indeed, Mammon and Wong had little choice but to fit into the shoes already laid out for them, given that their ethnicity was an inescapable aspect of who they were and what they did. As evidenced by the performance reviews by mainstream critics, the Chinese American artists and performers were never judged simply by merit. Invariably the critics pointed to the Chinese factor. When Jadin Wong and her partner, Li Sun, performed at the Fay's Theater in Providence, Rhode Island, they received this less than flattering review: "The dancing of Jadin Wong and Li Sun, though they are Chinese, doesn't vary much from the customary floor-show routine."[81] Another reviewer similarly could not separate their performance from the fact that they were Chinese: "The ballroom dancers of the week, Jadin Wong and Li Sun, are a pleasing Chinese couple but they seem a trifle out of their element in what one may presume are typical Occidental maneuvers."[82]

White America, generally speaking, saw the Chinese American performers as mere imitators of Western art. Accordingly, they were perceived as perhaps funny, cute, and dainty, but they were never taken seriously as artists. The performers saw themselves differently. Toy Yat Mar, who was called the "Chinese Sophie Tucker," did not much appreciate the name, since she did not see herself imitating anybody, but she stuck to it for commercial reasons.[83] As a self-fashioned artist, she subverted the expectations placed on her to be coy and shy with a dainty voice. Toy Yat Mar was, in fact, boisterous, loud, and funny. As Arthur Dong's documentary film *Forbidden City, U.S.A.* makes clear, these Chinese American entertainers were artists who defied the roles expected of them by both the Chinese and Anglo-American culture. They sang and danced to tunes that one does not usually associate with the Chinese.

Conclusion

The performers of the Forbidden City nightclub helped to expand the range of career opportunities for the Chinese in America. Likewise, Jade Snow Wong and Pardee Lowe, with the benefit of education, broke new ground by becoming artists, writers, and interpreters of Chinese America. Both the entertainers and the writers showed mainstream America that Chinese America was decidedly more modern than that of previous times. Thanks to the liberal racial logic of cultural pluralism, and the wartime patriotism that tended to diminish racial and cultural barriers, some Chinese Americans, encouraged by the new, relatively favorable image of the Chinese, stepped out and took center stage.

As cultural interpreters of China and Chinese America, Jade Snow Wong and Pardee Lowe provided commentary on subjects ranging from China's people, its paintings, pottery, literature, to its culture. Speaking from their position as insiders, they believed that they were giving a representational view of China and Chinese America. They felt no need to make clear distinctions between the culture of China and that of Chinese America. Their representation of things Chinese reverberated in the minds of those Americans who had already been exposed to the orientalist discourse of the Chinese.

While Jade Snow Wong and Pardee invoked essentialized notions of Chineseness in order to fashion themselves as cultural interpreters, entertainers in the Chinese American nightclubs, having grown up outside Chinatowns, distanced themselves from Chinese culture and the expectations it placed on young American-born generations. Showing that the Chinese could dance or sing as well as anyone else, they took up Western cultural forms. At a time when both mainstream America and the older Chinese community derided exposing the naked human form, some female Chinese American entertainers had no problems showing off their bodies. While many like Jadin Wong and Toy Yat Mar had hopes of making it big and being judged simply on their abilities, they found that the Chinese factor was an inseparable aspect of who they were as entertainers in the eyes of their white audience and critics. Some, like Mary Mammon, realized that in fact their success had much to do with their perceived

Chineseness. Like many others, Mammon knew that the success of Forbidden City had everything to do with it advertising an all-Chinese floor show. Crucially, Forbidden City was the lucky break that helped to launch the careers of many aspiring Chinese American dancers and singers. Knowing how to read the desires of their audience became a key component for ensuring their success. For Chinese American women, this sometimes meant catering to white male desire embodied in the image of Susie Wong or the Chinadoll. For others it meant knowing how to swallow their anger and the impulse to harm those in the audience who made taunting, racialized remarks. And yet within limits, these Chinese American entertainers subverted age-old images of the Chinese simply as laundry boys, shopkeepers, or restaurateurs, and found a niche within mainstream America as entertainers with a unique twist, capitalizing on their Chinese identity. And by distancing themselves from the cultural imposition of their Chinese elders, they earned a degree of freedom by pushing the boundaries of what it meant to be an American-born Chinese during the World War II era.

3

"To Become

Still Better

Americans"

The Challenge
of China Turning
Communist

China's gone to hell, but I'm still proud I'm a Chinaman. In America, if you sit in a corner and be quiet, nobody pays attention to you. You gotta stand up and say what you think and be yourself.

—Nee Wong, a vaudeville singer, 1950

"Today the doors are closed," stated Rose Hum Lee, a prominent sociologist who frequently wrote for the newspaper *Chinese Press*, referring to China having turned communist. She warned that the American-born generations "must learn to adjust themselves to the society here as never before." Their survival under these potentially volatile circumstances hinged upon the American-born becoming "a more integral part of the American society."[1] In 1949, when the defeated Nationalist Party led by Chiang Kai-shek retreated to Taiwan and the Communist Party leader, Mao Tse-dong, emerged as China's new ruler, Chinese America, although separated from China by the vast sea, was profoundly affected. Given the history

of anti-Asian movements on the West Coast, including the internment of Japanese Americans during World War II, Chinese Americans in California exercised extra caution in their relations with
white Americans. Public disavowal of communism and integration
into American society were the twin principles behind the native-
born campaign to guard against open hostility.

A marked shift in the image of the Chinese in America occurred
when the political climate underwent a transformation from a period of relative confidence in the 1940s to an era of insecurity and
fear in the 1950s. Communism loomed large in the American mind
as a threat to national security. The very fabric of American society
seemed to depend on keeping communism out. Like no other period
in American history, the fifties were marked by what David Caute
calls a certain "artificial straining and striving" for social and national conformity.[2]

The "loss" of China to communism came as a severe blow to
American confidence, as it was one among many other defeats
America suffered, beginning with the rise of Soviet Union as the world
leader of communism, its takeover of Eastern Europe, and its influence in many third world nations.[3] To lose China to communism
was particularly painful, as China had been a faithful ally of the United
States. China's sudden change of status from friend to foe caused
deep resentment, frustration, and anger in many Americans who,
only a decade earlier, had begun to see the Chinese as the friendly,
assimilable race. In China, the open-door policy for which Americans had historically fought long and hard had come to an abrupt
end; the door stayed open only long enough to eject the Americans,
whose presence and influence were no longer welcome. The American public came to regard the Chinese people with deep regret when,
despite the more than $2 billion spent supporting the Kuomindang,
China rejected America in order to take up with Soviet Union.[4] Be-
lieving that the Chinese were repaying American generosity with
evil, one career official at the State Department stated, "Because of
what we did while others were treating them badly, we think the
Chinese ought to be grateful to us. I run into this idea often, in our
way of writing about China policy, our acts in China, back to Boxer

days and John Hay. The Chinese should be grateful. That's why we're so riled up about Red China. That they should go and join up with the Russians makes us doubly mad."[5]

American resentment only increased when China became involved in the Korean War a year after becoming communist. The Chinese, according to Harold R. Isaacs, came to be described as "inhuman," "treacherous," and "deceitful, fighting hordes" who were killing "our boys." With China's new military role in international politics, the Chinese came to be known as a decidedly violent people.[6] The image of the Chinese as "warriors" capable of great cruelty and destruction came to replace a more placid view of the Chinese as moral philosophers. A congressman described how he came to see a more combative side of the Chinese emerge:

> I could not visualize the Oriental as a terrific, rugged, capable soldier. It was first brought home to me in Korea in 1951. Iron Mike O'Daniel told me the Chinese army was as well staffed and trained as any he knew. . . . Seemed strange for Chinamen, went against the whole idea I'd ever had of the Chinese. . . . I knew a streak of cruelty was there, but couldn't quite see them as the terrible, tenacious soldiers they turned out to be.[7]

Chinese cruelty became the subject of much discussion in the printed media. As evidenced by titles like "Chinese Torture," "Chinese Extortion Racket," "No More Blackmail," or "The Squeeze," many articles appearing in mainstream news journals sensationalized the torture tactics used by Chinese communists to extort money. *Time* reported that the Chinese who were known to have relatives in the United States were placed in concentration camps, and sometimes "lashed by ropes" and "tied to horses and pulled apart" in order to exact huge sums from their American relatives. Another piece in the *Newsweek* pointed to still other forms of unusual punishments used by the communist officials, such as chewing on broken glass and eating excrement.[8]

Actually, suspicion and dislike of the Chinese were part of a larger ideological development in the early fifties that came to link communism with foreigners. During the post–World War I years, communism came to be associated with immigrants and foreigners. The findings of a 1947 investigation conducted by the Department of Justice showed that out of 4,984 of the "more militant members" of the Communist Party, 78.4 percent of them were immigrants or the children of immigrants. In addition, another 13 percent had spouses who were of foreign ancestry. Such studies, as well as accounts of spies and defectors who were of immigrant stock, showed that communism was not American but foreign.[9] In 1951 delegates from the forty-eight states convened at the American Heritage Foundation to renew their pledge and to draft "a re-declaration of faith in the American dream." To toast the occasion, bells were rung not only as a symbol of their renewed commitment to the American dream but also as a "gesture of defiance to the Enemy"—the alien, the nonconformist, the other.[10]

In addressing the communist threat, President Truman stated that the "mission" of the government was to defend "national security" and to protect American democracy against "the worldwide menace of communist imperialism." A foreign policy founded on such a premise inevitably also played a significant role in shaping domestic policy.[11] Truman explained, "Our homes, our Nation, all the things we believe in, are in great danger." In choosing to fight for "freedom," the president declared that it was also a fight "for the right to worship as we please, in any church that we choose to attend, for the right to read what we please, and the right to elect public officials of our own choosing."[12] The evangelist Billy Graham also invoked religious imagery by depicting communism as the "Antichrist" or as "the satanic religion," which held sway not only among the immigrants but also over "a great segment of our people." In an article in the *American Mercury* in 1954, he wrote: "The mysterious pull of this satanic religion is so strong that it has caused some citizens of America to become traitors, betraying a benevolent land which had showered them with blessings innumerable. It has attracted some of our famous entertainers, some of our finest politicians, and some of our outstanding educators."[13] And yet, while communism came to be associated with all the ways of anyone who might not worship the Christian deity or who perhaps spoke in a strange tongue, Chinese Americans, who had been historically viewed as foreigners and heathens and whose ancestral homeland had turned communist, were more likely to be suspected of communism, for example, than persons who were assimilated Slavs or other whites.[14]

The unflattering characterization of the Chinese impressed upon the public mind often proved to have real consequences in the public arena. The growing suspicion that every Chinese was a potential communist heightened concerns over Chinese immigration. Popular literature harped on the danger of Chinese communist infiltration. There was much talk about the various illegal means by which the Chinese were entering this country. Although it was no secret that the Chinese had been coming into the country illegally for decades, in the 1950s Chinese immigration was perceived as a social "problem" worthy of closer examination. New attention, for example, was given to certain loopholes in the immigration policies whereby a Chinese with American citizenship could visit China and then claim the birth of a son in China, thus creating a "slot" for a "paper son" to enter America. The examination of registered births showed that many were "fictitious births." One article noted that a certain Chinese American, Huey Bing Dai of San Francisco, had been caught "fathering" some fifty-seven of these paper sons. The message behind these articles was clear: with so many illegal immigrants, the possibility of communist infiltration was all the greater.[15] A writer for the *Chinese Press*, I. H. Gordon, argued that it was the American "fear of the Chinese" in particular "the several thousand Chinese" who came as "treaty visitors—students, merchants, temporary visitors and others" becoming "naturalized citizens"—that increasingly undermined immigrants' rights.[16]

Indeed, immigrant rights suffered a general setback. The McCarran Internal Security Act of 1950 permitted the U.S. attorney general to detain any persons suspected of espionage or sabotage and whose actions might endanger national security. The act spelled a clear defeat for immigrants in that it allowed the attorney general to deport anyone thought to be harboring suspicious views and denied immigrants the right to become naturalized and voting citizens.[17]

Posing an even greater threat to the American-born was the

possibility of becoming interned. From the experience of the second-generation Japanese, the American Chinese understood that citizenship was no guarantee against the infringement of civil rights. As American troops experienced bitter defeats on the Yalu River battle front, between China and North Korea, Chinese Americans became ever more anxious as hostility and resentment grew against the Chinese. An editorial in the *Chinese Press* described the unfolding events in Korea as a "Pearl Harbor" for Americans of Chinese descent. For no apparent reason other than the "crime of ancestry," the Japanese, the editorial reminded readers, had been "swept out of their homes and locked in concentration camps."[18] Reports of increasing incidents of brutality against Chinese Americans in San Francisco signaled for Chinese Americans that not only mere words but even physical violence might be used against them. In conclusion, the editorial made a plea for an end to such hostility: "Despite these faint signs of intolerance which occasionally arises with uncomfortable swiftness in this country, . . . Chinatown, USA, faces the future with the basic hope . . . [that] this country will not let hysteria or prejudice flame uncontrolled again."[19]

At the end of 1951, an editorial reflecting upon the events of the preceding year and looking ahead to the next brought home a clear message and spelled out a policy for surviving these hostile times. "Be on guard," warned the editor. Even if the war in Korea should come to an end, as long as the march of communism continued and as long as the ancestral homeland of Chinese Americans remained communist, "eruptive public feelings" could work against them. He called upon the Chinese American community to continue their "good-will public relations" and to be "on constant alert." Chinese Americans must make all efforts "to maintain closer contacts with Caucasian groups," so as to dispel any misunderstandings and unwarranted suspicions against them.[20]

In their eagerness to prove their loyalty to America, Chinese Americans were willing to give up the practice of dual citizenship. Many native-born generations claimed both Chinese and American citizenship. The claim to exclusively American citizenship was in itself a pronouncement spoken in favor of America over China. Under such delicate circumstances, when their reputation as loyal American citizens was on the line, Professor Francis L. K. Hsu, an anthropologist from Northwestern University argued, the practice of maintaining dual citizenship only further jeopardized their position.[21]

> We must make clear whether we are citizens of China or America. A dual and ambiguous allegiance, an opportunity shifting back and forth between Chinese citizen and U.S. citizen, while at times advantageous to some individual, cannot but be harmful to the cause of natural development of Chinese American in the long run. All privileges, in the long run, are accompanied by corresponding obligations and you simply cannot eat the cake and have it. As of 1954, however, the Nationalist Government, wanting to free persons of Chinese ancestry from Communist claims, abolished the practice of dual citizenship. In light of this new ruling, maintaining dual citizenship might be interpreted to mean that one was sympathetic to Communism, thereby jeopardizing one's position as a loyal American citizen.[22]

The decision to give up Chinese citizenship, incidentally, echoed a move made a decade earlier by a number of Japanese Americans, who had given up their Japanese citizenship in response to the strong anti-Japanese sentiments. By 1954, the Nationalist government also came to see that it was in the best interest of the diasporic Chinese to give up the practice of dual citizenship, especially since the communist regime might try to make claims on the Chinese living abroad.[23]

To bolster their resolve to prove their loyalty and innocence, a group of young community leaders from the Chinese YMCA and YWCA and local churches in San Francisco drew up a list of tenets to be adopted as the official position of all patriotic Chinese in America. Some went so far as to post them on their doors and storefronts.

1. We Chinese-American citizens pledge our loyalty to the United States.
2. We support the nationalist government of free China and her great leader, President Chiang Kai-shek.

3. We support the United Nations charter and the efforts made by the United Nations troops who are fighting for a united, free and independent Korea.
4. The Chinese communists are the stooges of Soviet Russia. Those who are invading Korea are the Chinese communists, not the Chinese, peace-loving people of free China.[24]

To appease their non-Chinese neighbors, some promoted the view that communism was antithetical to the character and thinking of the Chinese people. Using examples from Chinese philosophical tradition, an editorial in the *Chinese Press* contended that communism as an ideal was foreign to China. To the contrary, China had long been dominated by a philosophical tradition of "democratic" thought. In fact, Mencius had taught—incidentally, before the birth of Christ—that "government is worthy only so long as it regards the people as the basic element in the state." Hence, the task at hand, the writer argued, was to "recapture" the original thinking of the "freedom-loving" Chinese by overthrowing the "foreign-led" masters of communism in China.[25] This argument articulated and corroborated the prevailing triumphalist view in mainstream America that democracy would eventually win out over communism. Such a view would have found an audience with those who found it impossible to accept the new view of the Chinese as the Reds. "I don't regard the Communist government as Chinese," stated one sympathetic to a gentler image of the Chinese. Others denied that the Chinese had any natural inclination for communism: "There isn't any China. It is now part of Russia," confirmed another.[26] Henry Luce, the head of *Time* Inc., concurred in this denial of reality and liked to tell his friends, "The only ambassadorship I would take is to a restored democracy in China." Given Luce's undying support of China's nationalist party, Chiang Kai-shek by the mid-forties had appeared on the cover of *Time* more often than Roosevelt, Churchill, or Hitler. [27]

Expressing a similar sentiment, Shavey Lee, who was called the unofficial mayor of New York's Chinatown, in answering the question put to him: "Are Chinese Communists the same as Russian Communists?" stated, "Let me emphasize that the Chinese people on the whole—and that means 99 percent of them—whether in China, America, or any other place in the world, are NOT Communists."[28] Still others made the distinction between the Communist rulers and the Chinese people. The editor of the *Chinese Press* explained that the few powerful Chinese leaders—mainly, "Mao Tse Tung and his Red Horde"—had fallen under Soviet imperialism and had forcefully imposed a foreign regime on the Chinese people. China had become a mere "Soviet satellite."[29]

Signaling a shift in the identity of American-born Chinese in the 1950s, a new term, "American-Chinese," came into vogue. While the term "Chinese-American" had been in use for some decades, it was deemed no longer appropriate, for it connoted, in Rose Hum Lee's words, "descendants of a racial and cultural group." Moreover, the term placed more emphasis on being "Chinese" than "American." But the most convincing argument for adopting the new term was that the former carried "an over-manifestation of loyalty to the Chinese group" that would undoubtedly lead to "criticism and questions regarding their place in the American society," stated Rose Hum Lee. The new appellation, American-Chinese, expressed primary allegiance to America.[30]

As American Chinese, Lee argued, one had a better chance of becoming more fully "transformed into a homogeneous part of the majority society's core culture."[31] A trained sociologist, Rose Hum Lee, played a prominent role in articulating and promoting the goal of assimilation to Chinese America. Having received her graduate training as a sociologist at the University of Chicago, she was a convert to Robert Park's theory of assimilation. Her 1947 dissertation, "The Growth and Decline of Rocky Mountain Chinatowns," was a study of her hometown of Butte, Montana.[32] Her personal story exemplifies a successful assimilation into American society. Rose Hum Lee, the second oldest in a family of four girls and three boys, was born into a wealthy merchant family in 1904. Along with her siblings, she achieved honors throughout her high school years. After a brief period of living in Canton with her husband, she was divorced and returned to the States with her adopted daughter, with the goal of continuing her education. Lee put herself through college at the

Carnegie Institute of Technology in Pittsburgh and then, some years later, resumed her studies as a graduate student at the University of Chicago. She became the first Chinese American and the first woman to head the sociology department at Roosevelt University in Chicago. Throughout her scholarly life, Rose Hum Lee observed assimilation patterns of Chinese Americans. In her own words, she was interested in "how the process of acculturation, assimilation, and integration operates when persons with distinguishable physical characteristics, bearing a different culture, come into contact with people of European origin."[33] Having so framed the problem of integration, she formulated a simple solution: the complete eradication of foreignness. By fully adopting the values and norms of the dominant society, one could hope to blend in and become indistinguishable from the rest. She urged her fellow Chinese Americans to do everything possible to "integrate" more fully into the American society. The culmination of her thinking is contained in her book *The Chinese in the United States of America*, published in 1960. Some of the views expressed in the book could also be found in the columns Lee wrote as a frequent contributor to the *Chinese Press*.

In her study of the diaspora Chinese, Rose Hum Lee observed that in some cases they "have become so integrated in the societies where they themselves or their ancestors settled that they are indistinguishable from the local population."[34] As for the Chinese in the United States, particularly as the American-born generations began to outnumber the "China-oriented" members of the community, nothing short of "total integration into American society" should be the "ultimate ideal to which all overseas Chinese should aspire."[35] By integration, Lee meant that the minority group in question should completely assimilate and adopt the norms, values, and traditions belonging to the dominant society. In so doing, the ethnic group necessarily gave up any distinctive cultural norms and practices that drew attention to its difference. Hence, apart from maintaining certain culinary habits, holiday celebrations, and the cultivation of the arts—none of which offended white America—Chinese Americans, she urged, should aim to resemble typical white Americans. Her use of the term "integration," then, is to be distinguished from the way it was used in the black civil rights movement.

The upwardly mobile, professionally inclined, American-born generations tended to applaud and to be guided by Lee's charge to integrate. Her authority in the eyes of the American-born generations lay in the fact that she had earned a Ph.D. and a position as the chair of the sociology department of an esteemed college. The *Press* never failed to mention the long list of accomplishments and degrees earned by Lee with every piece it printed by this author. Rose Hum Lee became a model for other American-born Chinese, particularly women, who desired entrance into the mainstream professional market. That her ideas were met with considerable opposition and scorn from the foreign-born generation was unfortunate but ultimately inconsequential to her, since she was confident that in time the American-born generations would outnumber them, thereby diminishing what she called the China-oriented influence and power. By 1960, she estimated, the former would easily constitute two-thirds of the total Chinese population.[36]

A move toward integration presupposed the move out of Chinatown. Lee encouraged the American-born generations to leave Chinatown for the suburbs. According to her assimilationist scheme, the disappearance of a discernible and distinctive Chinese ghetto would "increase amalgamation" with the larger society.[37] She called upon the young American-born generations to lead the exodus since they have "become acculturated and strive for higher status through education and enter professions or become employed by American industries."[38] Echoing similar sentiments, Richard Quil, another sociologist, urged the Chinese as a whole "to emerge" from their "Chinese wall" and move about "in the normal American social scene [and] to make contacts with other Americans." By implication, those who chose to stay behind in Chinatowns were said to be "cliquish" and unwilling to "extend their circle of contacts."[39]

The suburb was where a greater part of middle-class America had transplanted itself. During this period, suburban America grew forty times as fast as did the central cities, so that by 1960 the numbers in the suburbs equaled those in the cities.[40] Although some Chinese were able to move into the suburbs in the postwar years, the majority stayed in Chinatown due to residential restrictions and prejudice. The ban on housing restrictive codes in 1947, however, helped to facilitate the exodus, as those with the financial means bought homes in Oakland, Richmond, and Berkeley. Generally speaking, the elderly, the newer immigrants, and those occupying a lower economic echelon, stayed back, while the younger generation mostly composed of American-born generations who were in white-collar professions, some "stranded" Chinese educated in the United States, as well as rich merchant families, moved out.[41]

     Those who remained had a name for those who moved out: "avenue kids." Having left the crowded streets lined with graffiti-marked tenement halls, the suburbanites lived on wide, nicely swept avenues lined with trees and in individual houses with considerable breathing space between them instead of crowded multiunit apartments. The name "avenue kids" also connoted those with white, middle-class values. Indeed, many children of Chinese families living outside Chinatown spoke only English. As these children attended schools in predominantly white neighborhoods, they socialized exclusively with white Americans. Predictably, these suburban adolescents adopted white, middle-class values while keeping some superficial aspects of Chinese heritage; they came to be derisively called, by those who lived in Chinatown, "bananas"—"yellow" on the outside but "white" on the inside.[42]

     For some American-born Chinese, Chinatown came to represent a darker, bygone era. Jin Goodwin, a high school student, wrote an award-winning essay called "Come Out of Chinatown," which was published in the *Chinese Press*. She wrote, "Since our parents and grandparents were hounded into the depths of degradation by fear and intolerance, many younger Chinese have grown up fearing the white man, and allowed themselves to be beaten into feeling inferior—so much so, that the majority of them cringe and creep back further into the black depths of Chinatown, afraid to come out and prove that they can be a desirable element in American society."[43]

Life in Chinatown increasingly came to be viewed in negative if not pathological terms. "[Chinatown] is much too narrow-minded, inquisitive, and gossipy," complained a newly transplanted suburbanite, adding that the air in the suburbs was "much healthier and better. . . . You pick up too many bad habits there." He considered himself "lucky" for having moved out before Chinatown "corrupted" him. He vowed that he would never return to that "depressive atmosphere." Many American-born Chinese believed with Rose Hum Lee that "the number of Chinatowns" would diminish to a near "vanishing point," and consequently wanted nothing to do with what would, they believed, become a thing of the past.[44]

A clear socioeconomic distinction could be made between those who left and those who remained. The professional class tended to live in the suburbs and maintained wider contacts with the broader American society through professional and social organizations. Typically a couple living in the suburbs held college degrees. As in the average middle-class American white family, the wife usually stayed home while her husband became the sole breadwinner. A study completed in 1947 of Chinese American college graduates in California revealed that 81.6 percent of them were engaged in professional work, as compared to 16 percent in business and 2 percent in skilled labor.[45] In comparison, the merchant class, even if residing in better residential districts or the suburbs, nurtured ties and held membership in Chinatown-based organizations in order to boost their business. Both husband and wife worked in the family-owned business, usually late into the evening, leaving little time for leisure. In this way, socioeconomic position and lifestyle could be indexed by the relative distance to, and level of contact with, Chinatown.[46]

At the top of the economic hierarchy were those who had degrees from prestigious institutions of higher learning and had earned professional credentials as doctors, lawyers, theologians, physicists, chemists, and engineers. Just below the elite professional class were the social workers, architects, laboratory assistants, research associates, optometrists, draftsmen, nurses, and teachers in junior colleges or public schools. The level of professional and technical occupations rose from 2.9 percent in 1940 to 7.2 percent in 1950. Then there were the managers, proprietors, and executives employed by mainstream companies as well as bookkeepers and specialized white-collar workers. Below them stood the small businessmen who owned restaurants, beauty shops, and groceries. At the lowest level were those who stayed behind in Chinatowns working as garment workers, sorters, packers of food, truck drivers, waiters, cooks, laundrymen, domestic workers, and tour guides.[47]

The move to the suburbs signified not only a certain economic status but also an ideological orientation more conducive to becoming more fully integrated into American life. The suburban soil with its emphasis on social homogeneity and conformity became fertile ground for those desiring to look and behave like the Joneses. At the 1949 Lake Tahoe Conference of Christian youths, on the subject of assimilation it was agreed that the best way to bring about "a greater degree of understanding" between the races was for Chinese youths to "move out of Chinatowns." A move away from Chinatown metaphorically meant not simply "geographically" but also "traditionally"—that is, giving up old Chinese thinking and adopting American thought.[48] Corroborating a similar outlook, Rose Hum Lee stated that more than "race" proper, "ideology"—by which she meant one's worldview—"has loomed as a more important criterion" for joining the American society.[49]

Repressive Politics of the Cold War

Rose Hum Lee and the American-born Chinese of her generation, who zealously embraced integration, did so consciously or subconsciously in reaction to the broader ideology prevalent in the fifties Cold War era. At a time when any mark of foreignness came to be associated with communism, conformity in the guise of complete assimilation to what was considered normative by the dominant society appeared imperative for any ethnic group's survival, particularly if its members did not look "American." Hum Lee's plan for total integration, calling the minority group in question to consciously work toward obliterating any mark of ethnic distinction, made sense under the repressive logic of this period in the fifties. Social conformity became a necessary ideological underpinning for the way that social and cultural institutions in the United States came to be organized in the 1950s.

Sociologists David Riesman, Nathan Glazer, and Reuel Denney pinned a name to the personality type that would evolve from the socially repressive atmosphere in the 1950s. In their book *The Lonely Crowd: A Study of the Changing American Character* (1950), they wrote about an emergent character type called the "other-directed" personality who was the embodiment of sensitivity and tolerance, but whose "progressive" spirit ironically led him to sacrifice his individualism for the sake of conformity to a group. Such persons with the penchant for the "other-directed" personality were not likely to challenge their parents, their teachers, or their governing leaders. Their economic success depended not only upon how well they got along with their bosses and their peers but also on how they were able to fashion a successful public self-image.[50]

C. Y. Lee's popular novel *The Flower Drum Song*, published in 1961, echoed some of the convictions and values that gave rise to the "other-directed," upwardly mobile Chinese Americans in the 1950s. In the novel, capitalism is unabashedly celebrated and communism derided. Wang Ta, the main protagonist, persists with his medical studies instead of going to China, thanks to the advice of Uncle Chang. His uncle, a native of China, explains to naive Wang Ta the difference between a communist and a democratic society:

> You must realize that in this country perhaps you only refused the opportunity to do what you want to do; but in China you will be forced to do what you don't want to do. Let me quote some of Lenin's own words. "As long as capitalism remains, we cannot live in peace," he said. "The basic rule is to exploit conflicting interests of capitalist states and system. In doing so, we have to use ruses, dodges, tricks, cunning, unlawful method, concealment and veiling of truth." If you want to join their camp, you'll invariably be forced to do all these. As an honest man,

you cannot happily plunge into jobs that are entirely against your nature. . . . Communism and capitalism are like fire and water, they will never mix.[51]

In his speech, Uncle Chang affirms the belief that America is the land of limitless opportunity; and in such a system, blame for failure solely lies within the individual who does not seize the opportunity. Over time, Wang Ta comes to hold Western medicine in higher esteem than Chinese medicine. He decides to continue with his medical studies in order to establish himself as a doctor of Western medicine in America.

His career crisis notwithstanding, Wang Ta's deeper troubles lie with coming to terms with his liminal position as a Chinese American. Wang Ta's story mirrors the making of the other-directed personality described in *The Lonely Crowd*. He finds himself having to negotiate between extreme American individualism on the one hand and Chinese authoritarianism on the other. Even as he openly disagrees with his tradition-bound father, he remains the filial son. For instance, it is only upon the gentle coaxing of his son that Wang Ta's father finally decides to see a Western doctor for his chronic lung condition. And even as Wang Ta embraces the American principle of individual choice, he is not particularly spontaneous, innovative, or original. As evidenced by his career choice, his practical side wins over his more idealistic penchant. His even-tempered and tolerant disposition wins him more allies than enemies. Unlike his profligate younger brother, Wang Ta does nothing to jeopardize his social and economic standing.

Education as Key to Success

Wang Ta is typical of the emerging professional class of model American-born Chinese who sought success through education. A record-breaking number of 714 were enrolled at the University of California, Berkeley, in 1948. Of the total only 17 percent were students who had been born in China. Of the American-born group, 499 were men and 215 were women.[52] In the Western states, the majority of the graduates were American-born, whereas in the states east of California and Washington, they were predominantly foreign-born.[53] Judging from the kind of majors they chose—engineering, chemistry, public health, pharmacy, and architecture—they were obviously interested in those fields with the greatest promise of economic security in the mainstream job market.[54] In the year 1950, about 180 Chinese American students were graduated from these top institutions: University of California, Berkeley; University of Chicago, University of Pennsylvania, University of Washington, University of Southern California, University of Illinois, University of Michigan, Stanford University, and Northwestern University.[55]

While they were not blind to the existence of prejudice in the job market, a majority of the American-born still affirmed the importance of education for opening the doors of economic opportunity. On the subject of jobs, Rose Hum Lee encouraged the American-born Chinese to continue in their efforts to pursue higher educational degrees, in spite of the downward trend in professional job placements and the discrimination still operative in many fields. "Don't let your race get in the way," she advised. "We as a group often believe that others in the society fare better than ourselves." She pointed to a study conducted by her colleague Beulah Ong Kwoh, whose findings showed that on the average Chinese American college graduates earned higher incomes than average college graduates in the United States.[56] Besides, she firmly believed, the prejudice against the Chinese in the marketplace was a temporary phenomenon and that under "normal" times, "employment barriers" would become "relaxed" if not altogether "nonexistent."[57] Consistent in her integrationist logic, Lee promoted the popular view that anyone, regardless of race, could move up the economic ladder. Mirroring this sentiment, William Lloyd Warner, Marchia Meeker, and Kenneth Ellis wrote in their preface to *Social Class in America: a Manual of Procedure for the Measurement of Social Status*: "All of us are trained to know and to cherish the ideals of democracy and to believe in the American Dream which teaches most Americans that equal opportunity is here for all and that the chances for success for anyone lie within himself."[58] *Social Class in America* relayed to readers how they could gain expertise "in identifying any class level" of any person, based not on "half-knowledge and confused emotions of experience" but on scientific methods, which allowed for precise measurements.[59] The importance of knowing exactly where one (and one's neighbors) stood in the class scale, according to the authors, was not to instigate class conflict but rather to encourage upward mobility for all Americans. An article in *Life* magazine discussing the book underscored upward mobility as the distinguishing characteristic of American society: "The phenomenon of social 'mobility'—the opportunity to move rapidly upward through the levels of society—is the distinguishing characteristic of United States democracy and the thing for which it is famous and envied throughout the world."[60]

In their book, the authors set out to show how one could concretely measure the exact location of one's socioeconomic standing using such factors like occupation, income level, type of housing, location of home, level of schooling, dress, type of car owned, and so forth. Concurring with this rather sanguine view of class in America, the *Chinese Press* regularly showcased those who had achieved distinction in the academic or the professional realm. An editorial in the *Chinese Press* urged young Chinese Americans to increase their chances for economic success by practicing "more cautiousness in their choice of majors" so as to become trained in those fields that were more likely to secure them jobs.[61]

The world of medicine, high on the list of professions, was said to open up the doors of opportunity for Chinese Americans. This included general medicine, dentistry, pharmacy, and medical research, along with optometry and audiometry. So prestigious was the field of medicine that it was not uncommon to find the names of medical school students printed in the *Chinese Press*.[62] Other promising fields were said to be accounting, corporate law, estate law, and medical jurisprudence, as well as specialization in Chinese language, its people, and its culture, intended to serve the federal government. In the technological fields, sanitary engineers, radar experts, TV experts, physicists, biochemists, laboratory technicians, and highway engineers were listed. Teachers and social welfare workers were also in high demand. Given the variety of more lucrative fields to choose from, the American-born generations judiciously avoided the arts and the literary fields, as evidenced by school registries and the publication of graduate listings in the *Press*.[63]

The message brought home in all the advice about college and career choice was that one could counteract the negative forces of racial prejudice by working even harder to achieve distinction as a Chinese American. The listing of names of those graduating from prestigious institutions, as well as the showcasing of those who had won special honors, were regularly featured in the social columns of the newspaper, as evidenced by the titles: "Nine Chinese Win UC Scholarships," "Oakland Girl Valedictorian," and "Portland's Pride: Thora Lee Wing Wins $1,400 Vassar Scholarship."[64]

Chinese Americans Model Success

The efforts of these ambitious, American-born people to achieve academic honors and professional success must have impressed the general American public. Far from posing a threat to the American way of life, this segment of the Chinese American population rose in the general estimation as a model minority. Though the term "model minority" was not explicitly invoked until the late sixties, the notion of the hardworking, high-achieving, well-disciplined Chinese American youth first came into vogue in the 1950s. In addition to the glowing reports about their academic excellence, the supposed absence of juvenile delinquency was often cited as a generic trait of Chinese youths in America. A cursory review of the popular literature reveals that this view of the Chinese was widely publicized in the 1950s.[65]

The most commonly stated reason given for the lack of delinquency and crime among the Chinese youths was traditional respect for parents and the importance of the family over the interests of the individual. This popularized view of the Chinese gained greater currency when Francis L. K. Hsu wrote in the prologue to his *Americans and the Chinese: Two Ways of Life* (1953) that "the Chinese and American ways of life may be reduced to two sets of contrasts. First, in the American way of life the emphasis is placed upon the

predilections of the individual. . . . This is in contrast to the emphasis the Chinese put upon an individual's appropriate place and behavior among his fellowmen."[66] In New York City, *Saturday Evening
Post* reported that none of some 10,000 teenagers who had been ar-
rested were Chinese American. The point of the article was that
Americans could learn much from the Chinese.[67] A piece appearing
in the *New York Times Magazine* heralded the "wholesome" "family life" of the Chinese as the main reason behind the apparent absence of juvenile delinquency. Particularly admirable was that the
members of the family worked together with "unquestioned and
automatic" cooperation. The Chinese example put the rest of New
York City to shame, since juvenile delinquency in the general population was said to have risen by 32.5 percent in 1957 over the previous year.[68] The typical American family ruled by the philosophy of
individualism was largely criticized; Chinese youth, endowed with
the innate ability to understand well the limits of their freedom, appeared incapable of rebellion. William McIntyre of the *New York
Times* stated that this "healthy environment," which nurtured
"belongingness," also "establishes a safety limit on the inflation of
one's ego." "Thus it would be unthinkable," he opined, "for one to
adopt the braggadocian attitude of the delinquents."[69] Such a stereotypical rendition of the Chinese not only prescribed Chinese America
but also served to discipline the American youth and the society as a
whole, in order that its members might similarly learn to bow to
authority and to place themselves second to the more pressing common good of the family or the nation. Such a depiction of the Chinese
youth and community conveniently served the interests of the repressive state, which sought to discipline the public into giving its
primary allegiance to national, rather than personal or local, interests.

This highly idealized portrait of Chinese American youth and
the Chinese American community was, unfortunately, not drawn
from reality. Actually, juvenile delinquency in San Francisco's
Chinatown was becoming noticeably a great social problem. It was
no secret to the community residents that increasing numbers of
youths joining hoodlum gangs signaled a clear breakdown of traditional authority in the Chinese American community. "Hardly a

week-end passes," reported the *Chinese Press*, "without some dis-
ruptive incident and rarely is there a dance without these small gangs
spoiling the whole evening."[70] Between 1945 and 1949 there were 224
cases of juvenile delinquency in Chinatown, 210 involving American-
born Chinese. In an open letter to the editor, "H.J.K. from Berkeley"
stated that if the hoodlum gangs were allowed to continue to exist,
they would "reduce the Chinatown community to a chaotic, anar-
chic, and utterly despicable mess."[71] As a consequence of the bad
publicity ensuing from these hoodlum activities, businesses in
Chinatown experienced a slump. Art goods merchants, bankers, and
restaurant owners were the hardest hit. In the eyes of the Chinatown
community, these American-born youngsters, far from being model
sons and daughters, were troubled youths who had already "gotten
away with so much" and had badgered the community with their
violence and extortions.[72]

   While the merchants, and the older generation in general, tended
to blame the delinquent youths themselves, there were some among
the younger generation who pinpointed bigger causes behind the crime
wave. Annie Chan, a senior at a commerce high school, wrote an
award-winning essay on the subject of the "punk" problem in San
Francisco. She began by chiding the older generation, saying that
name-calling or blaming delinquent youths was not going to solve
the problem. Rather, better recreational centers and job opportunities for Chinatown youths were likely to yield more positive results.[73]
Indeed, unemployment among Chinatown youth had reached serious proportions. While statistics on unemployment in Chinatown
itself were not available, the *Chinese Press* obtained a copy of the
Department of Employment survey that revealed that employers were
reluctant in 75 percent of job orders to hire "Orientals."[74] In light of
these glaring facts, Chinese Americans had to perform mental som-
ersaults in order to hold on to the American dream.

Social Life of the Upwardly Mobile

   What one did for leisure was an important gage of one's socioeconomic identity. The social pages of weekly newspapers announced

numerous events such as proms, dances, private parties, sports events, and beauty contests; and advertised numerous nightclubs, bars, restaurants, movie theaters, and cafés where the young, American-born Chinese could socialize and find entertainment. One would be hard pressed to find anything distinctively "Chinese" about these social events. As confirmed by Rose Hum Lee, the American-born were much more influenced by what she called these "secondary contacts" provided by way of leisurely associations as opposed to the primary contact of family.[75] For suburbanite Chinese, these leisure activities provided the added advantage of enlarging their scope of friendship with white America.[76]

Particularly since their standing as loyal American citizens depended upon the nurturing of certain tastes, values, and practices associated with middle-class America, upwardly mobile Chinese Americans had an awareness of social class made acutely manifest not only in their choice of entertainment but also in their buying habits. Swept up by the post–World War II optimism that restored the pre-Depression belief in the American dream, suburban Chinese Americans were eager to prove their standing on the upper echelon of the economic ladder. For the upwardly mobile, the goal of assimilation was inseparable from their desire to make it economically in America. Characterized by a heightened penchant for pursuing material well-being and a preoccupation with socioeconomic standing, a majority of young Chinese Americans resembled many others in America who were inspired by postwar optimism. As such, they came to see America as the land of equal opportunity and a society where ethnicity was not an insurmountable barrier against economic mobility.

The Contributionist Logic

The belief in the fluidity of class went hand in hand with a view of America that emphasized the culturally and ethnically heterogenous nature of America. The following passage from *USA: The Permanent Revolution* (1951) was indicative of a mood that celebrated ethnic diversity: "Here is a town addicted to schottishes, another whose social life centers around a Norwegian harmony club, another that features Czech gymnastic festivals. Here is a town with a Chinese restaurant, over there a town with German verein, over there a town redolent of frijoles, that speaks mostly Spanish."[77] Reflecting on what was unique about the American experience, the authors concluded that in America "all cultures are cherished, interwoven, [and] modified."[78] The book provided a defensive response on the part of conservative social pundits to the oft-repeated criticism from the left about America's racism, opulent wealth, rampant consumerism, and the subsequent weakening of America's moral imperative and its meaning.

While celebrating cultural difference, the writers of *Fortune* magazine never questioned the supposed universal appeal of the traditional American ideals contained in the Constitution.[79] Rose Hum Lee never challenged the overtly imperialistic and ethnocentric perspective inherent in such a view but rather promoted the consonant perspective that, in essence, "race [was] no longer the barrier it once was."[80] She went further to suggest that one could turn it into an asset. As examples, Lee pointed to the American fondness for Chinese food and Chinese motifs in contemporary American furniture.[81] Cultural assets could be readily turned into commodities.

Virginia Lee, in her book *The House That Tai-Ming Built* (1963), described a Chinese American girl negotiating her identity at a time when America both emphasized conformity to certain "American" ideals and celebrated cultural diversity. Lin, the protagonist, and her brother are fourth-generation Chinese Americans who, as model minorities, possess impeccable manners and filial piety.

Lin's formation as a cultural contributor is derived from her close contact with her grandparents and her Chinese school. Her grandfather, the link to her ancestral past, tells her about her family history. In the retelling of her family genealogy, Lin describes a Horatio Alger–style success story, a rags-to-riches saga. Tai-Ming, her great-grandfather, came with nothing valuable in his pockets and went back to China a rich man through sheer hard work. During his stay in the mining country of the Sierra California, Tai-Ming apparently encountered no anti-Chinese mining laws or even the anti-Chinese miners' tax, and never saw the tragic deaths and the dreams of so many others vanish into thin air. If the early Chinese settlers appeared a bit docile, it was, as the narrator explains, because "the Chinese never retaliated, for they were by nature peaceful and yielding."[82] To harp on anti-Chinese legislation would detract from Lin's central purpose of playing the cultural ambassador, the one who enlightens the general public about Chinese art, tradition, and literature.

Much like Jade Snow Wong, Lin goes away to college, only to become better acquainted with the Chinese culture that she knows only instinctively from growing up in a Chinese household. Enrolling in Chinese art courses, she becomes an expert in Chinese pottery. She finds that in fact her acceptance into the dominant society is predicated on her playing the role of the cultural contributor. While a majority of Chinese youths in the 1940s saw themselves as cultural interpreters forming a bridge between two cultures, the cultural ambassadors of the 1950s were singly interested in making a one-way "contribution" to mainstream America. That is, the fifties saw Chinese culture turn into a highly commercialized entity within American consumerist culture. Chinese culture belonged purely to the realm of aesthetics.

When her uncle Fook presents Lin with a Chinese "pale blue brocade jacket," she decides to wear it with her Western-style black dress and her black high heels, symbolizing in dress what she adheres to in her everyday philosophy. When Uncle Fook protests that the mixing of Eastern and Western dress renders her not "authentic," she replies, "This is an expression of my soul, a bit of the East, and a bit of the West, I have always found so much to love in both" (144). She herself never questions in her own right what it means to be an authentic Chinese American, but, typical of the accommodationist response, simply follows the protocol already existing for how she may best address herself to mainstream America. On another level, Lin comes to passively succumb to the implicit limits placed on her as an "inauthentic" American. She quietly accepts the failure of her relationship with Scott, a white American, given the seemingly insurmountable barriers involved in an interracial union.

Reflecting a sentiment similar to that of Lin, some Chinese Americans believed that in order to be better equipped for enriching the American culture, those so inclined should take up the study of language and culture in greater numbers than in the past. Wang, a student at Stanford University, decided to study Chinese since he realized that the government needed "translators, especially in high security duties." Dr. Theodore H. Chen, a professor of Asiatic studies at the University of Southern California, stated that since increasing numbers of universities on the West Coast were expanding their course offerings in Far Eastern studies, American students of Chinese ancestry were being presented with an "unrivaled opportunity to aid in bringing about a better understanding of their ancestral land and at the same time make a real contribution to the complex and growing culture of the United States." In so doing, the professor believed, Chinese cultural studies would enhance and highlight the importance of "Asia to the United States."[83]

While some did heed the call to engage in Chinese cultural studies, others turned to the world of fashion. The *Chinese Press* praised two sisters who had made a name for themselves in Manhattan's fashion world, for bringing "a real touch of the orient to American costume." Another example of a Chinese "orientalist" was the interior designer who prescribed a formula for achieving that special "oriental feeling in lamps": "Whip up lively oxblood red or yellow brushed brass lamps with black trim. . . . A lamp in black bone China with antique gold trim and a gold antique taffeta shade could fit beautifully into eighteenth-century English or twentieth-century modern furnishings." Still another Chinese designer in the world of fashion was noted for her "bold architectural lines and oriental beauty of style." In all these ways, the cultural assimilationists made a plea, imploring white America to accept Chinese Americans into mainstream America, if not as equals, then as exotics with cultural knowledge or special talents. Chinese Americans became exemplary models in whom the marriage of a pluralist and a classless America found expression.

Conclusion

If the American-born Chinese appeared to believe rather uncritically in the American dream, it was perhaps because they had to be grateful for their fate in America, for somewhere in the back of their minds lurked the less sanguine possibility of being cast away, locked up, and interned as disloyal Americans. Their loyalist stance toward America was in large part a result of fear. Under the repressive politics of assimilationist thinking, Chinese Americans in the fifties felt compelled to prove themselves 100 percent American, particularly after China—America's onetime war ally—had turned communist in 1949. At a time when any opposition to racial discrimination was thought to be communist-inspired, Chinese Americans rarely spoke out about job discrimination or social segregation.[84] The fact of their Chinese ancestry only strengthened their resolve to remain silent and inconspicuous. Eager to shed the unflattering aspects of their ancestral heritage, more than two-thirds of the entire Chinese American population moved out of Chinatowns into suburbs.[85] Despite racial prejudice, American-born Chinese pursued degrees in higher education in greater numbers than in previous years with the hope that education would not only open the doors of economic opportunity but also guarantee them the social prestige and rank of bona fide Americans. So convincing were their efforts that they had achieved a more favorable status as model citizens by the late fifties. Given the choice between possible internment or accommodation, the majority of Chinese Americans chose the latter. Unlike the Japanese, the Chinese did believe that their actions could deter the *possibility* (not certainty) of being interned. For some that meant taking advantage of the consumerist thinking of the fifties and cashing in as cultural contributors; they turned their distinctive marks of cultural difference into commodities while distancing themselves from Chinatown proper.

4

"Claiming

America"

The Birth of an
Asian American
Sensibility

Chinamen are made, not born, my dear. Out of junk imports,
lies, railroad scrap iron, dirty jokes, broken bottles, cigar smoke.

—Frank Chin, *Chickencoop Chinaman*

"[A]sians face relatively powerless and circum-
scribed lives. We contribute in taxes or labor to the disproportionate
gain of others and accept as inevitable or unchallengeable (as do most
colonized peoples) our own limited horizons," began an essay col-
laboratively written by Asian American activists on the subject of
U.S. imperialism abroad in Asia and its link to racism against Asians
at home.[1] The writers concluded that, in light of U.S. involvement
in Southeast Asia, the most recent manifestation of the United States'
overstepping its powers, "there are useful analogies between the U.S.
treatment of Asians in Asia and the position of Asians in America"
(224). The belief that racism and capitalism were the twin evils perpetuating "some of the major ills borne by Third World countries
abroad and Third World communities at home" became the basis
for what came to be called the Yellow Power movement (225). Mark-
ing a radical shift in consciousness from the integrationist logic of
the previous two decades, the next two decades saw the rise of an

Asian American identity and culture that called for the repudiation of white culture and the rise of a new political and cultural identity.

This chapter examines the identity and the consciousness of native-born Chinese who, along with Japanese and Filipino Americans, established their roots in America by positing a revisionist reading of Asian presence in American history. In so "claiming" America, native-born Chinese Americans, Japanese Americans, and Filipino Americans became the advance guard of cultural and political activism that replaced the notion of the "oriental" with the "Asian American."[2] The call for "yellow power" was largely fueled by a series of nationwide protests beginning with free speech demonstrations, the black civil rights and the Black Power movements, followed by the anti–Vietnam War rallies. By the late sixties, Chinese and other Asian Americans found themselves swept up by the politically charged atmosphere.

Demographics

A unique set of demographic and social changes allowed the American-born generations of Asians to forge a unified coalition. The formation of the panethnic identity was made possible by the fact that by 1965, old national rivalries as well as the traditional cultural and linguistic barriers that had once existed no longer limited the American-born. Rather, the shared history of white racism became their common bond. Far removed from their ancestral ties, second, third, and fourth generations of Chinese and Japanese Americans felt more allied with each other than with immigrant generations. It also helped that the native-born populations came to constitute a majority for the first time in Asian American history.[3] With the majority of Asian America speaking English and comprising a significant segment of the young adult cohort, the college or university campus served as a fertile meeting ground out of which emerged various pan-Asian activist organizations such as the Asian American Political Alliance at the University of California at Berkeley. As William Wei argues, the Asian American consciousness and movement were largely instigated by middle-class, college-bound Asian Americans.

As Amy Uyematsu explained in her seminal essay on yellow power, the so-called identity crisis of Asian Americans, who no longer wished to ascribe to white norms and values, provided the crucial nexus that unified a generation of American-born Asians across ethnicities. They realized that self-contempt and confusion were natural responses to the disciplining and defining gaze of white America. The identity crisis was exacerbated by the fact that Asian Americans had largely adopted the illusory view that, if they would only follow the norms established by white America, they too might become fully American. Liberation required the rejection of such a false consciousness. Uyematsu stated that simple adoption of the norms, values, and sensibilities of white America did not guarantee integration into American society. She contended that the integrationist argument was essentially flawed.[4] "In the process of Americanization, Asians have tried to transform themselves into white men—both mentally and physically. Mentally, they have adjusted to the white man's culture by giving up their own languages, customs, histories, and cultural values. They have adopted the 'American way of life" only to discover that this is not enough."[5]

Similarly, Yuji Ichioka, one of the key founders of the Asian American Political Alliance and perhaps the first to coin the term "Asian American," concurred with Uyematsu by stating that Asian Americans for decades have painstakingly observed and mimicked "the behavior and mannerisms of white people." "We have tried to act like them, speak like them, look like them, and be like them in every way," stated Ichioka.[6] The name Asian American was in fact a repudiation of the term "oriental," which, as Huen explained, "was a name given to us by the West and it carried a set of cultural stereotypes which we came to reject."[7] Before Asian Americans could "define" themselves, Ichioka explained, they must first get over this "white hang-up."[8] In an open letter to the *Daily Bruin*, the UCLA campus paper, a young man by the name of Long spoke candidly about the "shock" of discovering that he was not white. "I am a white man," stated Long. "In fact, I get the shock of my life every morning when I wake up, look in the mirror, and see a Chinese man staring back at me." Another student, Wu, wrote in response to Long's letter: "No matter how an Oriental tries to become white, the white man will always look at him as being yellow and inferior!" Using the example of Long, Wu asserted that by "assimilating, Orientals are only prolonging and reinforcing the white superiority." Citing Long's confessional statement about his confused identity, Wu pointed to the tragedy and the ultimate futility of harboring self-deluding identities: "I see why he [Long] is surprised when he looks into the mirror, because if I were stripped of my identity, I too would be surprised."[9]

Implicit in this critique of the integrationist paradigm was also the rejection of the notion that Asian Americans as a whole constituted a "model minority." The model-minority trope can be traced back to the fifties when Chinese Americans were said to be hardworking, quiet, and loyal Americans. Chinese American youths were praised for lacking any signs of delinquency, and Chinatown leaders were praised for taking care of their own, without relying on outsiders' help. In the sixties, when the nation was plagued by racial strife, the so-called oriental success story served to appease Asian Americans and to discipline other racialized groups in the United States. By holding up Asian America over against other racialized groups, the model-minority thinking tended to pit Asians against other Americans.[10]

Some Asian Americans interpreted the model minority thesis as yet another manifestation of the mythical passive oriental. Uyematsu interpreted it as an invitation for some to achieve a modicum of economic and social standing at the expense of other colored groups. The model-minority myth promoted the thinking that America was not "fundamentally racist."[11] Moreover, she pointed to the ways in which such a thinking obscured the fact that "racial discrimination toward yellows" continued to exist "in upper wage level and high-status positions."[12]

Although the native-born Chinese population had made some economic gains since the 1940s, they were far from standing on equal footing with white Americans. The 1970 census showed that while there was significant improvement in the area of professional and technical jobs, with 26.5 percent of the native-born Chinese male population employed in these fields as compared to the rate of 2.8

percent in 1940, it must also be noted that 15 percent of the native-born workforce made their living as owners or operators of small businesses such as restaurants, gift shops, or grocery stores.[13] Given their high level of educational attainment, many of the American-born Chinese were typically underemployed. Only 13.3 percent of Chinese American males with four years of college had personal incomes of $10,000 or more in 1970, as compared with 27.7 percent of white males with the same number of years of college.[14]

Underemployment was also a common phenomenon for native-born Chinese females, who were overwhelmingly situated in clerical jobs as bookkeepers, cashiers, secretaries, office machine operators, typists, and file clerks. More than 40 percent of Chinese American female secretaries had college degrees, as compared to the great majority of white females working as secretaries, who had only high school degrees. In California, 36 percent of the gainfully employed, native-born Chinese females were clerical workers or operatives.[15]

Influence of the Black Power Movement

As model minorities, Asian Americans were expected to follow the norms and values of white America and to shun the ways of black America. The reverse was the case for some Asian Americans who in fact found that they had more in common with black America, with whom they shared the experience of racialized Americans. Asian American students at the University of California at Berkeley and San Francisco State College were particularly moved by the Black Panther Party, founded in Oakland in 1966. Its critique of American imperialism, repudiation of white values, and call for self-determination influenced much of the thinking behind "yellow pride" and "yellow power." Amy Uyematsu explained that the principal thinking behind the Asian American movement, "race pride and self-respect," were "direct outgrowths of the Black Power movement."[16] Jean Quon, who participated in the Asian American movement in the late sixties was profoundly influenced by personages like Frantz Fanon, who wrote *The Wretched of the Earth* (1963). In reading this book, Quon found the "crucial link" between "political struggle and the emergence of a new identity." "In the late sixties, we gained not only a bit of political freedom but also a new understanding of ourselves and what it meant to be Chinese or Asian American. It meant the beginning of a new consciousness," said Quon. Having seen stark pictures of racial inequality between blacks and whites during the days of the civil rights and the Black Power movements, she recalls, "You couldn't help but be affected by it, when you saw the dramatic events of the movement unfold before your very eyes on television every night."[17] Alfred Wong, who was attending San Francisco State at the time, found intellectual mentors in figures like Fanon and in Stokeley Carmichael, the coauthor of *Black Power: The Politics of Liberation in America* (1967). Wong explained that there was a direct correlation between what "the third world countries" were trying to do "in terms of their economic, political, and cultural independence," and "the self-determination for Asian Americans."[18] Implicit in his analysis was the belief that the struggles of third world people paralleled those of racialized minorities within the United States. Asian Americans, along with other racialized Americans, saw themselves as "internal colonies" engaged in the struggle to liberate themselves from the systematic cultural, economic, and political oppression of the white hegemonic society.[19]

The Vietnam War

During U.S. involvement in Vietnam, Asian Americans had come to believe that Asian lives counted for little in the eyes of white America. Many Asian Americans interpreted U.S. intervention in Vietnam as an act of racism against the Asian people as a whole. Ampo Fusai, a UC Berkeley student, wrote in the Asian American Political Alliance news magazine that the American presence in Vietnam was nothing more than "the perpetuation of the white man's war of colonial exploitation and the bloodletting of Asian peoples."[20] As Laureen Chew, a participant in anti–Vietnam War demonstrations, explained, "an increasing number of Asian American college and high school students realized with a shock that the enemy whom American soldiers were maiming and killing had faces like their own."[21]

Seeing unarmed, unresisting civilians napalmed in Vietnam angered young Asian Americans. Asian American protesters were not shouting "give peace a chance" or "bring the GIs home"—a rallying cry among white antiwar protesters—they for their part were proclaiming "stop killing our Asian brothers and sisters" and "we don't want your racist war."[22] At a symposium called "Towards an Asian Perspective on Vietnam," in the fall of 1969, the focus was not on the lives of American soldiers but on the Vietnamese people's struggle for liberation.[23] Following the meeting, more than three hundred Asian Americans took part in a noon rally that began at the Peace Pagoda in Japantown and ended at the Polo Field in Golden Gate Park.[24]

Through their participation in the antiwar movement, Asian Americans strengthened their sense of pan-Asian solidarity. Increasingly they came to realize that as Americans of Asian ancestry they were bound by a shared fate, a predicament sealed by a legacy of white racism and imperialism. To their mind, the oppression of the Asian people living in America was not at all different from the colonizing projects in nineteenth-century America or from America's involvement in Vietnam. The pan-Asian coalition thus came to be overtly identified by a racialized identity. Allying themselves with other "internal colonies" within the United States, they also began to support third world movements. On the UC Berkeley campus, Asian American students joined the Third World Liberation Front in pressing the institution for ethnic studies courses.

Activism on Campus

Asian Americans on campuses like UC Berkeley and San Francisco State College demanded an end to institutional racism. They pointed to their thoroughly Eurocentric education, which related little that they considered useful to the surrounding ethnic communities. They reasoned that education must be responsive and relevant to the needs and concerns exigent in their communities. Self-determination for themselves and an education that responded to the needs of their communities became the principal aim of the student movements on campuses on the West Coast. In concrete terms, their goal was the establishment of autonomous ethnic studies programs that would make racialized Americans the focus of their study. Students themselves wanted control in hiring faculty and in curriculum development in this educational project inspired by cultural nationalism.

Floyd Huen, who attended UC Berkeley during the ethnic studies protests, reasoned that "because the university had for so long served the needs of the white dominant community, it was about time it attended to the welfare of ethnic communities."[25] As the president of the Chinese Students Club (CSC), consisting mostly of American-born Chinese, Huen talked about how he "involved" the university by using the club stipend to run fieldwork programs. With university funds, he set up a field office in the basement of the International Hotel in Chinatown, ran a shuttle service from Chinatown to campus, paid for publication costs of newsletters, and provided gas money for commuting students. He added proudly, "We didn't pay a cent out of our own pockets."[26]

Jean Quon, reflecting on her thoroughly Eurocentric education, realized how little she really knew about the history of Chinese people in America. Though she had always known that she had ancestors in America as far back as the late nineteenth century, she did not learn until she came to Berkeley and spoke with other "conscienticized" Chinese Americans that "the Chinese exclusion laws were largely responsible for the ghettoization of the Chinese" in dilapidated Chinatowns. In fact, many heard about Asian American history for the first time at conferences such as the one sponsored by the Chinese Students Association and the Nisei Club on the Berkeley campus. An unexpectedly large crowd of about five hundred young Asian Americans attended the Berkeley "Yellow Identity" Conference in January 1969, not only eager to learn of their history but also anxious to talk and to share with one another their experiences as persons of Asian ancestry. Typical of such gatherings, the conference featured speakers such as Stanford Lyman, who lectured on the history of the Chinese and the Japanese in the United States; Paul Takagi, on America's foreign policy in Asia; and George Woo, on the social and institutional structure of Chinatown.[27] Many spoke publicly about their identity as Asians for the first time. Laureen Chew, who participated in the student strikes at San Francisco State, told the story of this pivotal time in her life.

> One Friday evening, a fellow Chinese American student came up to me and asked if I would like to go to a talk. She said that it was a talk on racism. I asked, "What racism?" And when she said, "The way the white people treat the Chinese," she didn't have to say any more. Having gone to an all-white Catholic high school, I knew what she meant. At the talk, I found myself nodding to every word spoken. Suddenly I realized that nothing was wrong with me. I'm not going crazy. What I had been experiencing all along was "racism." At this conference, I was able to give a name to this feeling inside of me.[28]

This "awakening" gave Laureen Chew the feeling of seeing with a new pair of lenses. When she observed the university, she now saw an institution set up by the "white man" "to civilize" the minorities "by their Western standards." Russel Leong, a Berkeley student, wondered how such an education could be "relevant" to Asian Americans.[29] Jean Quon questioned what a degree from Berkeley might mean to a Chinese American: "I had an uncle who got an engineering degree from Berkeley in the thirties only to become a grocer in Chinatown."

Having reached "the limits of [their] tolerance," many Chinese Americans began to seek "new alternatives" to an "irrelevant" educational system. They resolved to join the Third World Liberation Front (TWLF) to reform the academic agenda on the Berkeley campus. Chinese students, as part of the Asian American Political Alliance, joined the Front, uniting with the Afro-American Student Union (AASU) and the Mexican-American Student Confederation (MASC) to strike against the university, which was reluctant to meet their demand for a Third World College. Asian American students, the largest minority on campus, became a strong and vocal component of the TWLF. In 1968, San Francisco State College was the first to have established an ethnic studies department in the country; by the fall of 1969, the University of California at Berkeley also established an ethnic studies program.[30] By the early seventies, over fifteen campuses in California and some on the East Coast had recognized the need for courses in Asian American experience.[31]

Core members of the Asian American Political Alliance busied themselves with the task of designing Asian American courses. A course called "Yellow Experience" provided an overview of the history, culture, and contemporary life of the Chinese, Japanese, Filipino, and Korean Americans. Another course examined student movements in Asia, such as the Cultural Revolution and May Fourth Movement, and the Red Guard movement in China, and the overthrow of the Korean government in 1954. A third course examined "the profound impact Western civilization has had on Asia."[32]

Transforming Chinatown

Activism on campus led naturally to community activism. In an open letter to the Chinese Students Association (CSA), printed in the *Daily Californian*, the Berkeley campus newspaper, an anonymous writer threatened to transform the "social" club into one more concerned with community issues. The author of this letter accused club officers of steering the group merely toward social activities such as "parties, picnics, and beauty contests" at the expense of doing more "meaningful" and "much-needed welfare activities" in Chinatown. Since the club was predominantly comprised of foreign-born students from Hong Kong, who were less inclined to get involved with domestic concerns, the anonymous writer argued for their involvement in Chinatown, because many of those in need of help were also newly arrived immigrants, and Chinatown was just across the bridge.[33]

The following week, Ronald Lee, a representative of the CSA, wrote a face-saving response promising that CSA members would be "planning a definite push toward expanding social programs in the Chinese community." The change had come about, he explained, largely from "more of the membership" becoming increasingly "aware and concerned" as "evidenced by unsolicited letters to the CSA."[34]

To demonstrate its new commitment, the CSA participated in a public forum on conditions in Chinatown. Actually the second in a series, this forum touched on matters of housing, senior citizens, and the Chinese community structure. This across-campus affair drew students from San Francisco State College, San Francisco University, San Jose College, and Stanford University. "This event was the first project which involved the Chinese American students on a large scale," commented Ling-chi Wang, a graduate student and a key organizer of the forum.[35]

In the late sixties, the Chinatown that these Asian American students revisited was sorely dilapidated. Over the years, Chinatown had increasingly turned into a place for the elderly and the impoverished. There was "no mistaking the fact that it [San Francisco's Chinatown] [was] a ghetto," stated Buck Wong, a graduate student in history at the University of California, Los Angeles, given the slumlike, overcrowded conditions wherein over forty thousand people were crammed into only forty-two square blocks.[36] In 1960 a third of all Chinese in America lived there. The internal structure provided little for the welfare of its people, and the outside institutions had abandoned it altogether.[37] Sparked by a deep desire to change Chinatown, Chinese American students sought to use their educational institutions to ameliorate conditions. For some who knew firsthand what it was like to grow up in Chinatown, going back to Chinatown was a chance to right a childhood wrong. Having grown up in a place that was mainly a tourist attraction, Ben Tong explained, he had come to regard Chinatown with humiliation and shame. He was particularly resentful of white tourists. "It was the way they looked at you," he said.[38]

> Now it is a strange thing, but lately
> the Deadly Devils have been walking the streets
> in January of all months. I mean
> it ain't even summer and they're here.
> It's too cold for Hawaiian shirts and cut-off
> pants. But we know them by the way they force you
> off the sidewalk and bug you about,

"Where is there a good place to eat, son?"
And there's always one Deadly Devil who knows
Some Chinaman back home—"A great guy,
so hard workin', gracious, quiet, and funny."[39]

A white tourist staring into the gates of Chinatown saw "a little China," a land of "100 million miracles" as described in *Flower Drum Song*—a Hollywood movie hit in 1961—or, according to another tour guide, "a mystical land of Buddhas, jade, silk, carved ivory, herbs and bazaars," with benign-looking restaurateurs, who, incidentally, were always laughing, surrounded by dancers and singers who were not only extremely attractive but also full of charm and dexterity. All in all, Chinatown was an enchanting place.[40]

"Chinatown as fantasy-land for the whites" was how Laura Ho, the editor of *Gidra* (a monthly published by students in southern California) described it. Just like Disneyland "[Chinatown] exists to please white America," she wrote. But in fact, the white tourists "forget that real people live in it." Ho explained that this image of Chinatown came to her while she listened to S. I. Hayakawa, president of San Francisco State College, speak before an audience of Japanese Americans in Disneyland. Hayakawa spoke of San Francisco's Chinatown with glowing compliments, precisely in the way *bok gwai* tourists did, and Hayakawa went so far as to add that it was a place "all Chinese can be proud of."[41]

"The truth is, beyond the façade, Chinatown is really nothing more than a gilded slum," countered Gordon Lau, a young attorney who served as president of Concerned Chinese for Action and Change (CCAC), an organization comprised of students from San Francisco State College and UC Berkeley along with a few lawyers and clergy.[42] "Flower Slum Song" was a tune familiar to the students. San Francisco Chinatown was full of destitute and lonely people. About 41 percent of Chinatown's fifty thousand people lived in poverty according to federal standards; the population density was 885.1 per residential acre compared to the citywide average of 189 per residential acre; about eight thousand new Chinese immigrants moved into Chinatown looking for schooling, jobs, and housing every year; more than 21 percent of deaths in Chinatown were caused by tuberculosis, which was no less than three times the rate for the rest of the city. There were more than 150 garment factories where many women worked for twelve to fifteen hours a day, for less than a dollar an hour. The 1960 census revealed that the average person over twenty-five years of age had only 1.7 years of formal schooling. Meanwhile, the high rate of juvenile delinquency was caused in part by the enormously high unemployment rate of 12.8 percent, compared to the citywide rate of 6.7 percent. Finally, 67 percent of the housing in Chinatown was considered "substandard," compared to 19 percent for the rest of the city.[43]

Chinatown provided for the young American-borns a clear example of how the racist and imperialist designs of the dominant white society had destroyed an ethnic community. They learned how the Chinese had been excluded from the mainstream economy and society, exploited as cheap labor, ignored by social and welfare services, and made to feel culturally inferior to the dominant race. In the sixties, the garment industries exploited the labor of Chinese women. Chinatown was indeed an internal colony—an ethnic island within the borders of America that existed primarily to benefit the dominant society.

By demonstrations, protests, and their writing, American-born Chinese decried the grim reality of conditions in Chinatown. Suddenly Chinatown was beginning to receive unsolicited attention in the press. The *San Francisco Chronicle* ran a four-part series on the conditions in Chinatown in the late summer of 1969, and the *Los Angeles Times* followed with a story on the radical changes taking place in Chinatown. By the late sixties, there was a notable decrease in the type of reporting and writing that portrayed Chinatown as a "fantasy-land."[44]

"There was just so much to do," recalled Jean Quon, who worked as a volunteer tutor in Chinatown. The Asian Community Center (ACC), located in the basement of the International Hotel, offered tutoring in English, math, and the sciences; a counseling program for the immigrant young; and a free food program. Founded by the Berkeley students in 1970, the center also served as a field office.[45] In the same building, the students ran a special project, a sewing school. Their intent was to "teach the immigrants sewing skills," explained Bryant Fong, "so that eventually they will own the entire production process." Fong explained that this school was set up as an "alternative" to the "unions and garment factories that exploit the workers."[46]

Though the capitalist "outsiders," such as those who set up garment factories to take advantage of cheap labor, were partly to blame for exploiting the Chinese, the old guard—that is, those such as the Six Companies, the monied merchants, and the tongs, who exerted a powerful influence over affairs in Chinatown—were equally at fault for perpetuating poverty and exploitation in Chinatown. Young community activists, such as Gordon Lau and Ling-chi Wang, viewed the old guard as the biggest obstacle to improving Chinatown.[47] "If the leadership here," commented Lau, referring to the old guard, "isn't concerned about the neglected working man, the forgotten juvenile and overlooked senior citizen, how can we criticize the non-Chinese for not responding to our needs?"[48]

Originally the clan associations functioned as a necessary and beneficial system that offered assistance and protection to a clan or a village, otherwise neglected by the central Chinese government in the nineteenth century. Similarly, left to survive on their own in America, Chinese communities naturally came to rely on the services of their family or clan associations not only for protection but for their livelihood as well.[49]

Over the years, however, an informal political structure developed around these clans, whose leaders wielded power through attaining wealth and catering to the interests of the elite—factory owners, merchants, and landlords. Hence a variety of benevolent associations, trade guilds, and secret societies came to constitute political units, which tried to extend their influence and power by enlisting more people to join them. More concerned with the loyalty and cohesion of their members than with their welfare, the traditional ruling elites became more exploitative than protective.[50]

The preservation and solidification of the informal political structure in Chinatown was made possible partly by the policy of nonintervention on the part of the U.S. government. Historically, the dominant society conveniently stayed out of Chinatowns, reasoning that the Chinese knew how to take care of their own. Because it was not accountable to any external ethical or legal system, the informal political structure easily deteriorated into partisan politics, serving the interests of the ruling elite. Meanwhile, the concerns of the average waiter, grocer, laundry worker, factory worker, and cook in Chinatown went unmet.[51]

Increasingly, the young Chinese Americans came to view the old establishment as obsolete, an anachronistic institution continuing despite the changed needs and concerns of Chinatown in the sixties. An editorial in the *East/West Magazine* made fun of the Chinese Six Companies' attempt at addressing the poverty issue. While it was heartening to see the Six Companies "so excited over the anti-poverty program," it was rather "ironic" that not one of the participants at the meeting "appeared to be poor," wrote the editor. When asked why the poor were not represented, one participant was quoted as saying, "Ordinary poor people were invited but, I guess, they're too uneducated and just didn't come." The editorial ended by insinuating that if the Six Companies were serious about solving the problem of poverty, they would "put down some of their thirty million which they owned in properties alone."[52]

Alan Wong, a San Francisco State student who was one among many bringing the struggle into the community, remembered that the friction between the students and the old guard became at times severe. "The conservative groups in Chinatown reacted" to the student activism, recalled Wong, "by making up stories that we were Hong Kong students trained by the Red Guards to upset Chinatown's relationship with the white community." Some of the old guard "threatened to have immigration authorities investigate" the families of the activist students. Such threats, however, only worked to show that in the end, "they were afraid of us because we were now equally strong in the community."[53]

Contrary to the convictions of the activist youths, the "establishment" did not welcome bringing "outsiders" into Chinatown or involving the community in mainstream city politics. And least of all did they appreciate young activists "airing their dirty laundry."[54]

When the young Chinese American activists began setting up welfare agencies and social centers in Chinatown, they challenged the entrenched informal political structure.

Working in Chinatown opened the eyes of these activists, not only to the political structure and hierarchy, but also to how the community functioned in the larger society, as well as their own role in it. Laureen Chew found that although she had lived in Chinatown all her life, she "never really understood how it worked" until she became a community activist.[55] Gordon Lau found "working with the people a very humbling experience." Although Lau was culturally a Hawaiian Chinese and far from being perfectly bilingual, he felt that some of the Chinatown old-timers took him in and "considered him one of their own."[56] Jean Quon learned a valuable lesson about the way society functioned: "I saw poverty in a different light. I grew up poor myself. My mother could have probably qualified for welfare. . . . But I never really understood the institutional and political nature of poverty until this time."[57]

Asian American Women's Movement

While racial oppression was the rallying cry for social change and the assertion of yellow power during this period, Asian American women began to question whether the exclusive attention to race placed them in a position subservient to the men in the movement. Asian American women, who were active participants in the antiwar movements and in the sit-ins for ethnic studies, began to see that even as the men worked toward racial equality, they were less than conscientious in their treatment of women. Laureen Chew discovered to her dismay that even the "movement" or "activist" brothers treated women in a condescending manner. "There were only about five of us who were actively involved. . . . We women had very little decision-making power," said Chew.[58] "We did all the shit work, but that was not an issue at the time." Jean Quon recalls that she was particularly "put off" by the men who modeled themselves after the Panthers, since they acted very "macho." She remembers how her group, AAPA, was generally "more egalitarian" than many other groups, but still when representatives were chosen to appear before the academic senate or the chancellor, they were almost always men. Women tended to do the clerical and secretarial jobs. Quon's position as editor of the AAPA newsletter gave her much "power," but, she states, hers was an exception to the rule.[59]

In the early seventies, Asian American women who had witnessed the second wave of the women's movement take hold among white middle-class women also began to reflect upon their "doubly oppressed" condition as women of color. While many were inspired by the white women's movement, they were quick to point to differences. Asian American women had their own set of concerns to work through. Those who were affected by the new feminist consciousness realized that they must first come to terms with self-contempt. "We began by talking about the years of scotch-taping eyelids to create a double eyelid fold, then carefully painting it over with heavy strokes of Maybelline black liquid eyeliner," recalls Miya Iwataki.[60] In a society where white women were the norm for feminine beauty, Asian American women tried desperately to disguise their Asian features by peroxiding their hair, Scotch-taping their eyelids, and curling their eyelashes. Pam Lee talks about how every time she looked into the mirror she saw a "flat-nosed," "short-legged woman," and how she felt "inferior to white women." She also points out that Miss Chinatown contests epitomized the way Asian Americans had internalized white standards of beauty. Invariably, the women who were chosen were exceptionally tall, with high-bridged noses and large eyes.[61] Nellie Wong, an activist and poet from Oakland, describes what it was like to grow up comparing herself to white women in a poem, "When I Was Growing Up."

> When I was growing up, people told me
> I was dark and I believed my own darkness
> in the mirror, in my soul, my own narrow vision.
> When I was growing up, my sisters, with fair skin got
> praised for their beauty, and in the dark
> I fell further, crushed between high walls.[62]

In their discussions, Asian American women realized that matters of race and gender were intermeshed in inextricable ways. Within their Asian ethnic communities, women had to contend with the Confucian tradition that idealized subservience as a feminine virtue. Women were expected to be filial daughters and submissive wives bound to domesticity. Margaret Woo explains that within the West, Asian American women were orientalized as the ultrafeminine "Susie Wong, geisha, dragon lady, and Nancy Kwan."[63] And yet, Asian men too suffered from degrading, emasculated stereotypes. Woo stated that the image of the Asian man conjured up characteristics that rendered him unattractive and unmasculine.

> Asian Men are small skinny egg head emotionless flat nosed 98–pound weakling hairless chestless sexless short lifeless serious humorless practical cautious passive socially inept spoiled mommy's boy bucked teeth big lipped greasy hair tight eyed S.I. Hayakawa Engineer doctor Ph.D. accountant pool playing gay guy neuter Charlie Chan laundry man gardener houseboy hard working egotistic waiter The white man is depicted as the very opposite. White men are big muscular intelligent sexually powerful hairy tall fun easy going light colored hair eyes skin athletic aggressive dominating U.C. Penny Lincoln layer business man executive banker Joe Namath John F. Kennedy Jesus Christ.[64]

Even as women spoke rationally about the ways in which these stereotypes were socially constructed by the dominant society, they nonetheless could not help but be affected by them. Over time these stereotypes had indubitably produced a noticeable strain between the sexes. Wilma Chen spoke about one activist man, for instance, who was quoted as saying that he was all "for women's liberation," his only regret was that in the process, the women "lost a lot of their femininity."[65] Some men openly spoke of their preference for "blond, blue-eyed chicks," as described in a poem by Ron Tanaka: "I hate my wife for her flat yellow face and her soft cucumber legs, but mostly for her lack of elegance and lack of intelligence compared to Judith Gluck."[66] In turn, many Asian women confessed that they had low opinions of Asian men because they fell victim to the dominant society's racist stereotyping of them.[67]

The Cultural Meaning of Asian America

While the term "Asian American" was largely politically motivated, it also implied the birth of a new cultural sensibility as evidenced in the writings of this period. More than any other period in Asian American history, the sixties and early seventies saw a considerable outpouring of literary production by Asian Americans in such journals and magazines as *Amerasia Journal, East/West, Gidra, Yellow Journal,* and *Bridge,* among others.[68]

A reading of the works of three writers of this period—Frank Chin, Shawn Wong, and Maxine Hong Kingston—unveils the cultural significance behind the Asian American consciousness and identity.

Frank Chin's "Chinaman"

Frank Chin, along with Shawn Wong, Jeffery Paul Chan, and Lawson Fusao Inada, edited *Aiiieeeee! An Anthology of Asian-American Writers* (1974), which was intended as a manifesto of the emergent "Asian American sensibility." They wrote,

> Asian Americans are not one people but several—Chinese Americans, Japanese-Americans, and Filipino-Americans. Chinese and Japanese-Americans have been separated by geography, culture, and history from China and Japan for seven and four generations respectively. They have evolved cultures and sensibilities distinctly not Chinese or Japanese and distinctly not white American. Even the Asian languages as they exist today in America have been adjusted and developed to express a sensitivity created by a new experience.[69]

Pointing to a pivotal shift in consciousness, this cohort of Asian Americans did not see themselves as inheriting the best of the East and the West, but rather as occupying a unique position as Asian Americans. "Distinct" is the operative word that appears repeatedly in the description of their position as being not white American and not Asian. In contrast to the autobiographical writings of Pardee Lowe and Jade Snow Wong, among others, they insisted upon a radical break from the tradition that tended to accommodate rather than challenge the orientalized worldview of the East and the West. In retrospect, they argued, "This myth of being either/or and the equally goofy concept of the dual personality haunted our lobes while our rejection by both Asia and white America proved we were neither one nor the other."[70]

What constituted the Asian American sensibility was described only in the negative. Chin and company explained that the "Americanized Chinese" writers Lin Yutang and C. Y. Lee, who were "intimate with and secure in their Chinese cultural identity," were "American by choice," for, as evidenced in their writing, they "consciously set out to become American" in the "white sense of the word."[71] They played the role of the "good, loyal, obedient, passive, and law-abiding" "Chinese-American."[72] Frank Chin saw Lin Yutang, the author of *My Country, My People*, as currying favor with whites by painting an exotic and at times humorous picture of the oriental. C. Y. Lee was similarly criticized for having written the novel *The Flower Drum Song* (1961), which, to Chin's thinking, painted a rather unrealistic, glorified picture of Chinatown as the preserve of ancient, Chinese elite culture. Chin insisted that as an American-born, he had little knowledge of or concern with traditional Chinese culture. He was at pains to distance himself from the foreign-born Chinese. In an open letter responding to Ching, the editor of *Bridge*, who charged that Chin had gone too far in insisting upon the distinction between the immigrant and American-born Chinese, Chin explained why he chose to distance himself from Chinese immigrants.

> I am not shunning immigrants. I'm stating the fact that I am not Chinese. . . . As far as I'm concerned Americanized Chinese who've come over in their teens and later to settle here and American-born Chinaman have nothing in common, culturally, intellectually, emotionally. And it's the racist admonition that all Chinese be alike . . . because of skin color . . . and only that binds us together, sets us at each other's throats to work together for some form of white acceptance."[73]

Furthermore, he argued, "no cultural or psychological bridge" connected him to Chinese immigrants like C. Y. Lee or Lin Yutang, and only "social and racist pressures connect" them to each other.[74] The cultural nationalist position articulated by Chin et al. wanted nothing to do with the ancestral homeland, its people, or its cultural heritage.

The nationalist consciousness that emerged in the late sixties and prevailed through the seventies made a radical break with China of the past and the present. Unlike the nationalists of the 1930s who responded to the political turmoil in China, Chinese Americans of this period had little to say about the cultural revolution in 1963 or about President Nixon's visit to China a decade later.

As a "Chinaman," Chin ascribed to a different set of sensibilities. Unlike what he called the "David Cassidy" of Chinese American literature, who in being "white-washed" and all too "respectable" reeked of self-contempt, Chin was a "Chinaman" who was not ashamed of being simply Chinese in the way that a black militant was not afraid of being simply "black." Proudly reclaiming a name that was once derogatorily used to refer to Chinese cheap laborers, Chin presented this "third choice" rooted in self-pride and not "the fear of the whites."[75] This deliberately masculinist rendition of the Chinaman identity has to be seen in light of the long history of emasculation of Chinese men.

In *The Year of the Dragon*, a play written and produced by Chin in 1974, the protagonist, Fred, works as a tour guide in Chinatown. Living and working in Chinatown, all he can do is think about leaving. He tells his father that his job is killing him. "I've been sick and dying for ten years," says Fred to his father to which his father responds, "You my son. You lib my house. Meck my money. Tecking cares you China mama. Be Chinese now jolly time all finish."[76] As much as he would like to walk away from Chinatown, Fred's father is dying, and Fred feels the tug of the responsibility placed upon him by his father and his entire family. Chinatown is depicted as a place for the dead and the dying. In his fit of anger, he shouts, "I am shit. This family is shit. Chinatown's shit. You can't love each other around here without hating yourself" (124).

His contempt for his family stems from the fact that it offers him no enabling role models. From his American-born mother, he stands to inherit the Chinese America of Jade Snow Wong. Ma reminds him, "Don't forget you Chinese of American descent. Remember Jade Snow Wong" (92). His father offers him little more than the dubious privilege of being his Chinese, "responsiboo" son, which translates into supporting his family and the newly arrived China-Mama. China-Mama is so named as she is the first wife of Fred's father, who, like so many Chinese immigrant laborers, could not bring his wife into the country prior to 1943, due to anti-Chinese immigration laws. China-Mama also stakes a claim on him as her son. At every chance she reminds Fred, "Ngaw hai nay hug man," which means "You are my son" (92). This is more than Fred can bear: "You want me to be Chinese too, huh? Everybody does. . . . You know how the tourists tell I'm Chinese? No first person pronouns. No 'I,' 'Me' or 'We.' I talk like that lovable, sissy, Charlie Chan, no first person personal pronouns, and instant Chinese culture. . . . Ha, ha, ha. . . . I'm not Chinese. This ain't China. Your language is foreign and ugly to me, so how come you're my mother?" (115) Fred's rejection of the immigrant Chinese mother is rooted in the realization that she represents for him what the white racists see in him. Hence his rejection of her is rooted in a deeply felt contempt for what she comes to represent. He is unable to see who she is apart from how the mainstream society depicts the Chinese immigrant.

In Chin's short stories "Food for All His Dead" and "A Chinese Lady Dies," Chinatown is similarly described as a dark landscape where the old are dying and the young are helplessly watching them die. The young protagonist, Dirigible, in "A Chinese Lady Dies," finds himself in a position similar to that of Fred in *The Year of the Dragon*. He speaks in an internal monologue as he assists his dying mother in the bathroom: "I'm a nobody. I'm embarrassed with your condition. I mean, here I am a body, a meaningless part of the human economy, and I have a mind, but I really don't have anything to think about, I'm not particularly respected and don't have any self respect, not that that's bad or good, it isn't anything, here I am, not uncomfortably getting along with another who's dying."[77]

In *Chickencoop Chinaman*, Tampax Lum answers Dirigible's

challenge by leaving Chinatown and finding a niche as a newspaper reporter/writer working on a story about his boxing hero. Gaining some distance from Chinatown, he is better able to explore and experiment with various roles and to try on new styles. His tone and voice are infused with a self-mocking sense of humor missing in the characterization of Fred and Dirigible. Tam describes to a Hong Kong airline stewardess how a Chinaman came into being:

> Chinamen are made, not born, my dear. Out of junk imports, lies, railroad scrap iron, dirty jokes, broken bottles, cigar smoke. Cosquilla Indian blood, wino spit, and lots of milk of amnesia. . . . Born? No! Crashed! Not born. Stamped! Not born! Created! Not born. No more born than the heaven and earth. No more born than nylon or acrylic. For I am a Chinaman! A miracle synthetic! Drip dry and machine washable.[78]

Implicit in this description of the Chinaman is the insight that identity is not something you inherit, as from a father to a son, but rather it is a social construction. Tam distinguishes himself from the characters Fred and Dirigible, who cannot see identity as a form of invention. And yet, even with the benefit of this liberating insight, Tam still remains troubled. His childhood fantasy hero, the Lone Ranger, turns out to be a racist who shoots him in his writing hand. His real-life heroes turn out to be fake. And the memory of an old dishwasher, presumably his father, who bathed in his underwear, presumably because he suffered from emasculation, still haunts him. A father so ashamed of his masculinity, to the point of being unable to unveil his masculinity in his private moments, had apparently failed to become a positive role model for Tam, who is himself a poor father. Tam says to himself, "Chinamans do make lousy fathers. I know. I have one" (23). And as for his own kids, he states, "I want 'em to forget me" (8).

The play projects the vision of a generation of orphaned American-borns who are searching for a meaningful role model and a language with which to give birth to their newly emergent identity. Tam states, "I speak nothing but the mother tongue bein' born to none of my own, I talk the talk of orphans" (8).

Shawn Wong: Claiming America

The narrator in Shawn Wong's novel, *Homebase* (1979), is left orphaned at the age of fifteen and embarks on a journey to re-member himself to the family of his past. Early in the novel, Rainsford Chan introduces himself as a fourth-generation Chinese born in America. "I am a son of my father, my grandfathers, and I have a story to tell about my history."[79] Unlike Maxine Hong Kingston's woman warrior, he does not look beyond the American West for his roots. By beginning with the story of his great-grandfather, who built the railroads in the Sierra Nevadas, he is staking a claim on America. Rainsford is himself named after a mythic place in California, a town once peopled by Chinese. By establishing a strong and powerful presence of ancestral fathers in America, he lays claim to America as his very own. Rather than seeing his orphaned condition as a state of weakness, he models himself after his heroic ancestors, whom he describes as "the original fatherless and motherless immigrants" (7). He credits the Chinese great-grandfathers who toiled to build the railroads and worked the mines, with the making of the West. As a metaphor of their continuing, powerful presence, he recasts the land as extensions of their bodies laid to rest.

In the end, he re-visions the American West peopled with heroic "Chinamen" (69). By creating his own legends and myths, he rewrites the history of America in order to make it more than just a "home." "After 125 years of our life here, I do not want just a home that time allowed me to have." To claim America as truly his, he must "take myths to name this country's canyon, dry riverbeds, and mountains after my father, grandfather and great grand-father." Given four generations of Chinese presence in America, he states that they are "old enough to haunt this land" like "an Indian who laid down to rest and his body became the outline of the horizon. See his head reclining, that peak is his nose, that cliff his chin, and his folded arms are summits." The personhood becomes the place of America much in the way that the massive roots of the redwoods, which recur often in his dreams, become one with the soil (86).

Maxine Hong Kingston: The Woman Warrior

No novel expresses more poignantly the struggles of a young American-born trying to come to terms with her Chinese ancestral heritage and the tug of mainstream America than Maxine Hong Kingston's *The Woman Warrior: Memoirs of a Girlhood Among Ghosts* (1975). The novel could be read as a personalized meditation on the meaning of being an Asian American woman in the late sixties. Like Laureen Chew and Jean Quon, the narrator informs the reader that she is a product of the sixties: "I went away to College—Berkeley in the sixties—and I studied and I marched to change the world."[80] From a young age, the protagonist, the woman warrior, realizes that being born a female and a Chinese doubly marginalizes her in both mainstream America and Chinese America. Even as she asserts that she wants to become "American normal" (102), she repeatedly returns to the stories of her parents and her Chinese ancestors. In the end, it is the stories from her mother that nourish her sense of self. Her prodigal aunt, the one who might have "combed individuality" (10) into her hair becomes the nexus for figuring out her own identity as a Chinese American woman. The autobiographical novel begins with the narrator recounting the tale of her aunt. Rather than live with the lifelong insult of an unforgiving village, her aunt, accused of illegitimate pregnancy, drowns herself and her newborn daughter in the family well. Her mother tells her this story when she starts to menstruate, to instill in her the importance of chastity. The story causes her to desire to know more about the aunt who committed suicide, but her mother refuses to tell more and instructs her to be silent, never to speak of this aunt again. The secrecy with which her immigrant parents guard their existence leaves the girl confused. Kingston writes, "Those of us in the first American generations have had to figure out how the invisible world the immigrants built around our childhoods fits in solid America" (6). At times it seems that the immigrants deliberately set out to "confuse their offspring" who perhaps "threaten them" by always "trying to get things straight, always trying to name the unspeakable" (6). Her mother's injunction to silence makes her all the more eager to learn about her aunt's life and about how it "branches" into hers (10). While

Frank Chin emphasizes the disruption and the break between the immigrant and American-born generations, Kingston moves in the opposite direction, seeking to reconnect the bond between them, made tenuous by cultural, linguistic, and generational differences.

A distinguishing characteristic of her parents is their apparent lack of "frivolity." Compared to their children, who "flew kites," watched Betty Grable movies, and ate melting ice-cream cones, the parents allow only "the useful parts" to flow into their lives (6). The village that would not condone adultery has also produced Chinese immigrant parents who come to represent "necessity, the riverbank that guides [her] life" (6). The lack of extravagance, she comes to understand, has less to do with their being Chinese than it does with their being impoverished immigrants. She pays for her extravagant experience of a carnival ride with the "guilt" incurred, watching her "tired father" counting his change "on the dark way home" (7). In her fantasies, she becomes a woman warrior who avenges her poor family by attacking the racist bureaucrats who want to tear down her parents' laundry to make room for a public parking lot (57). While a great cultural and linguistic divide separates her and her parents, what binds them together is that they share the experience of the same "white racist boss. . . . I easily recognize them—business-suited in their modern American executive guise, each boss two feet taller than I am and impossible to meet eye to eye" (57). The woman warrior goes to battle against the white bosses of America by turning herself into the mythic Fa Mu Lan, a Joan of Arc of China, who disguises herself as a man to take the place of her aged father in battle. The traditional tale of Fa Mu Lan, as recounted in this novel, serves as an apt icon of this generation of American-born Asians who, in spite of the vast differences between their own and their parents' generation, became the filial daughters and sons who, for their parents' sake as well as their own, protested and marched to change a racist society.

Conclusion

Like no other time in Asian American history, the sixties saw the rise of a generation of Chinese and Japanese Americans bound together by political necessity, demanding that they be recognized not as orientals but as Asian Americans. In renaming themselves, they were consciously rejecting a long legacy of cultural stereotypes associated with the term "oriental." In one sense, by using the no- menclature "Asian"—which categorically lumped all people of Asian ancestry together—they were replacing one racialized term with an- other. An alternative view, however, is that the American-born Asians appropriated the term for their own political ends and, in so doing, infused it with new meaning. Much like Black Power, the notion of Yellow Power, often used to describe the new sensibility, referred to the wholesale rejection of Anglo-American values, norms, and tradi- tions and the adoption of a cultural identity neither wholly Asian nor white American, but occupying a "third space" that was said to be uniquely Asian America. Insofar as their roots were said to lie in America and not in China or Japan, they were "claiming" America as their own.

The process of claiming America was much like an archaeologi- cal expedition. The late sixties' politics of identity began with the recovery of identity buried and repressed by the legacy of imperial- ism. Once it was retrieved, the newfound identity was worn like an emblem, displayed like a trophy, in order to proudly assert a presence not previously acknowledged in public. And yet, while it was easy to say with certainty what was false—mainly, white depiction of the Chinese or the Asian—it was harder to say, at this point, what con- stituted a "true" image of Asian Americans. Frank Chin could only describe the meaning of Asian American sensibility by describing what it was not. Moreover, the explicitly masculinist construction of the Asian American sensibility, symptomatic of the cultural na- tionalist spirit of the sixties, refused to recognize the voices of women and the articulation of their experience. Insofar as the poli- tics of identity of the sixties and the seventies was very much rooted in the assumptions of modernist thinking, its subsequent insistence upon the distinctions between what was mere stereotype or false versus what was true or "real," or the prioritizing of race over gen- der, would prove to be needlessly self-confining and disabling when it came to deal with heterogeneity.

5

"Punching Our

Way Out"

Beyond Asian
American Identity

Do I have to explain why "exotic" pisses me off and "not exotic"
pisses me off? They got us in a bag, which we aren't punching
our way out of.

—Wittman Ah Sing in Maxine Hong Kingston,
Tripmaster Monkey

"[W]hat in the world is an Asian American?" ask
the parents in Gish Jen's novel *Mona in the Promised Land*, capturing the crisis of meaning behind the term "Asian American."[1] While
the novel takes place in 1968, today the legitimacy of this term has
grown slimmer still, given the growing heterogeneity within Asian
America. Indeed, the face of Asian America in the 1980s and the
1990s has changed considerably from that of previous two decades.
In the sixties, the Asian American community was predominantly
composed of American-born, English-speaking Chinese, Japanese,
or Filipino Americans. In 1960, 53 percent of Asian Americans were
Japanese, 20 percent Filipino, 1 percent Korean, 1 percent Asian Indian, and 27 percent Chinese. In 1985, 21 percent of Asian Americans were Chinese as compared to 21 percent Filipino, 15 percent
Japanese, 12 percent Vietnamese, 11 percent Korean, 10 percent Asian
Indian, 4 percent Laotian, 3 percent Cambodian, and 3 percent

"other."[2] The ratio between the foreign-born and the American-born population has also changed. Looking specifically at the Chinese American population, while the native-born constituted 61 percent in 1960, by 1990, the foreign-born dominated, comprising more than 70 percent of Chinese Americans.[3]

The Immigration Act of 1965, which allowed unprecedented numbers of Chinese immigrants to enter, played a factor in upsetting the population ratio between the native-born and the foreign-born. It permitted 170,000 immigrants from the Eastern Hemisphere per year, allowing 20,000 persons per nation. Exempt from the quota were family members of American citizens.[4] Chinese immigrants have come from Taiwan, the People's Republic of China, and Hong Kong. The Chinese came to constitute the second largest immigrant group, after Mexicans.[5]

The globalization of capital is another important aspect that has instigated the emigration of a diverse array of Asians and Chinese specifically. Recent studies of new Chinese immigrants show that they come not from only Hong Kong, Taiwan, and the PRC but also from Southeast Asia, Latin America, and Africa. The great ethnic diversity among the diaspora Chinese is matched by their economic variance. Occupying all echelons of the economic ladder, Chinese immigrants can be found in medicine, small businesses, engineering, and science; they occupy high-level executive positions in the Pacific Rim trade and production, and low-level occupations working alongside Latino immigrants.[6]

Given the more auspicious economic circumstance in contemporary Asia, American-born Chinese, along with other Asian Americans, no longer have to bear the stigma of being associated with a politically weak and economically destitute ancestral land. Unlike those who in the late sixties distanced themselves categorically from their foreign-born relatives, Chinese like other Asian Americans in the 1990s—particularly the progeny of post-1965 immigrants— embrace a diaspora identity negotiated between the Pacific Rim and the United States. Indeed, China, along with many other Asian nations, occupies a different location in the geopolitical realignment between Asia and the United States. Due to the rise of Japan and

China as world economic powers along with the "little tigers of Asia"—Korea, the Philippines, Indonesia, and Taiwan—the growth of transnational corporations, the collapse of communism, and the cybernetic transfer of capitalist culture, Asia no longer operates under the patronage of the United States, but as a partner in what Susan Koshy calls a new "borderless" economy.[7]

Within the United States, a set of ideological changes distinguish the racial climate of the nineties from that of the late sixties and seventies. While Chinese Americans engaged in the Asian American movement contended with the logic of integration, Chinese Americans of the eighties and nineties find themselves having to answer to the liberal ideology of multiculturalism as well as the neoconservative integrationist logic, albeit slightly revised from that of the sixties. The integrationists of the post-sixties era arose out of a backlash to the perceived threat of the group-rights movements; hence it embraces a constitutional return to individual rights and radical egalitarianism. Integrationists reason that, since individuals are no longer hampered by institutional and structural forms of racism, thanks to the Voting Rights Act of 1964 and the Civil Rights Act of 1965, there is no reason that "ethnic" Americans cannot assimilate culturally and economically into the core of what is implicitly understood to be Anglo-America.[8]

Such sentiment is strongest wherever there is a high concentration of Asians. In Monterey Park, California, where the Chinese constitute more than 50 percent of the population, the resentful white populace places pressure on the newer Chinese arrivals to conform to the ways of Anglo-America. In spite of the white protest against the non-English-language street signs and storefronts, there is little evidence that the Chinese in Monterey are assimilating. To the contrary, the proliferation of Chinese shops, social organizations, and newspapers points to the likelihood that the Chinese, according to Timothy Fong, are "taking over" the community.[9]

On the liberal front, multiculturalism poses a challenge for Chinese Americans who feel the need to punch their way out of categories. While multiculturalism does recognize cultural diversity and goes so far as to authenticate the cultural marginalia from an institutional standpoint, in the process, the identity of the "ethnic" Chinese other, in this case, easily becomes fixed to a referential sign consisting of an immutable set of practices, traditions, and meanings. In response to the homogenizing and universalizing discourse of multiculturalism, some of the American-born generation have come to embrace in the eighties and nineties what David Hollinger calls the "postethnic perspective." This orientation acknowledges that individuals occupy several positions simultaneously. Hence one may be said to be a Chinese ethnic, a woman, unmarried, a business owner, a Democrat. It is in the process of consciously and critically locating herself within these various layers of "we's" that the postethnic self is to be distinguished from the universalist.[10]

The postethnic may still choose to emphasize her ethnoracial affiliation not because communities of descent determine her primary identity, but because she is committed strategically to the renewal and critical revision of her ethnic community.[11] That is, insofar as racial prejudice still exists in the social and economic realms, and acts of violence are targeted against Asians in America, many are reluctant to do away with the term "Asian American," even as people feel the need to break out of the Asian American mold.[12]

Even as the American-born Asians find themselves represented in the upper echelons of the job market, they must still struggle with underemployment and inferior wages, compared to comparably skilled whites. In the 1990s, Asian Americans are most likely to be employed in managerial and professional specialty jobs. In 1996, 35 percent of the nation's employed Asian and Pacific Islander men and 31 percent of women sixteen and over worked as store managers, engineers, dentists, teachers, lawyers, and reporters. For Asian and Pacific Islander men, this was the most common occupational category, while it was second to technical, sales, and administrative support jobs for women. [13]

The preponderance of Asian Americans in professional jobs speaks to their high level of education. By 1990, 38 percent of Asians in the United States had graduated with a bachelor's degree or higher, compared to 20 percent of the total population. Nearly one-seventh of the thirty-two thousand doctorates awarded by U.S. universities in

1995 were conferred upon Asians and Pacific Islanders. This group accounted for roughly one-third of the doctorates awarded in engineering and one-quarter of those conferred in the physical sciences.[14] In spite of these gains, Asian and Pacific Islander men twenty-five years and older who worked year-round, full-time, and had median earnings of $41,220, earned about $87 for every $100 of earnings by comparable white men. [15]

Beyond Asian American Identity

In the eighties and nineties, Chinese Americans, along with other Asian Americans, have come to realize that they must go beyond the identity politics of the sixties. The pan-Asian American identity that arose out of a political need in the sixties threatens to dissolve under the vast economic and ethnic diversity within Asian America. Chinese American writers and activists focus on the need, on the one hand, to be extricated from the neatly ascribed stereotypes, embracing the postethnic perspective on identity, and on the other, to fill in what I call "the missing content" of culture, poignantly realized but left largely unfulfilled by the Asian American movement of the sixties and the seventies.

This chapter moves beyond the environs of California and examines the writings of Chinese American authors at large, so as to sample the diversity of opinions that continue to shape the culture and identity of Chinese America. While a great variety of writings by Chinese Americans exist for this period, I give primacy to texts written by previously discussed authors Maxine Hong Kingston, Shawn Wong, and Frank Chin along with other, new writers, since I want to explore how their thinking about Chinese or Asian American identity has changed since the sixties.

The Chinese American texts examined here discursively reflect upon the material conditions of prevailing ideologies; they also show how individuals navigate their identities within their confines. The texts reveal both a tendency to focus on the social construction of racial stereotypes (Maxine Hong Kingston) as well as the urge to go beyond racializing discourses in the hopes of establishing a distinctively

Asian American cultural legacy (Frank Chin). Writers such as Shawn Wong and Gish Jen reflect upon what Peter Kwong has labeled "the uptown Chinese," those who have moved out of downtown Chinatowns and moved up socioeconomically into suburbs, while Chin and Fae Myenne Ng speak about old-timers who decided to stay. Issues such as interracial marriage, the gender rift in Asian America, and generational conflicts are revisited in the texts of the eighties and the nineties.

Deconstructing the White Gaze: Tripmaster Monkey

Wittman Ah Sing in *Tripmaster Monkey* (1989) is engaged in a process of negotiating an identity more complicated than that of the young protagonist in *The Woman Warrior* (1975), who confesses to being unable to sort out for herself "what is Chinese tradition and what is the movies?"[16] Wittman, in fact, understands that notions of the East and the West are ideological constructions of the West. He is a postethnic seeking to transform the ways in which Anglo-America has marginalized and stereotyped the Chinese, by exposing the process of stereotyping itself. As a postethnic, Wittman Ah Sing defies any stereotypical rendition of the typical Chinese American male. He is iconoclastically outspoken and is enamored with Gypsy culture and flamenco.[17] Wittman gives unsolicited readings on buses and trains, choosing from a surprising variety of texts—ranging from those of Walt Whitman, Rainer M. Rilke, Mark Twain, Steinbeck, Jack Kerouac, and Carlos Bulosan, to relocation diaries of Japanese American internees.[18] He himself is an aspiring writer whose goal in life is to fill up his trunk, inherited from his vaudeville actor-parents, with poems and plays. Those familial linkages, however, belong to a distant past. He is in reality an orphan, restless and homeless, always coming in conflict with a society that has already named him. No matter what he does and how he tries to educate the public, he is constantly being misconstrued. Having to live under the imprisoning gaze of others, Wittman comes to possess a missionizing desire to change the way people perceive the Chinese. Wittman turns into an artist with a cause.

Wittman Ah Sing steps up onstage in the middle of his play to explain to his audience that they got it all wrong: "Stop the music— I have to butt in and introduce myself and my race. 'Dear reader, all these characters whom you've been identifying with—Bill, Brooke, and Annie—are Chinese—and I am too'" (34). Breaking up regularly scheduled performances, Wittman engages in guerilla warfare with his audience, holding them hostage to his vitriolic, Hamletesque so- liloquies. Creating discomfort, even shock, is an integral part of his performance art. Wittman accuses his readers/audience of normaliz- ing racist assumptions. He wants to "spoil" their "fiction." He tells them, "You have been sucked along, identifying like hell, only to find out that you'd been getting a peculiar, colored, slanted, p.o.v. 'Call me Ishmael.' See? You picture a white guy" (34). He wants to make strange what is normal and normalize what is rendered strange. "I am sore and disappointed," begins Wittman, referring to the re- views of the first opening night of the play. The reviews reinscribe the orientalizing rhetoric of East meets West replete with demean- ing culinary references like "snaps, crackles, and pops," and "sweet and sour." Getting to the heart of the critique, he declares, "There is no East here. West is meeting the West." Speaking with increasing bitterness and anger, he continues, "Do I have to explain why 'ex- otic' pisses me off, and 'not exotic' misses me off?" Wittman con- cludes, "They've got us in a bag" (308), and he wants to punch his way out of it.

He also chides his fellow Asian American actors for not going far enough in demanding nonstereotypical roles. Charley and Nanci, members of his theatrical troup, are quick to defend themselves, stat- ing that they've played more than the overtly stereotypical roles. Nanci says that she played a nurse once, and Charley boasts that he even had parts in the soaps. To which Wittman sardonically replies, "Did you play the lab tech again, Charley? Or the court stenogra- pher? You guys are too grateful. The job of the characters they let you play gets upgraded from criminal to servant to semi-professional, and you're fooled that we're doing better" (310).

Wittman is the "master of change" (306). As such he is not happy merely supplying the apparatus of cultural production. He wants to change the apparatus itself.[19] For instance, Wittman entertains the notion of transforming theater to re-create community. He says, "Community is not built once-and-for-all; people have to imagine, practice, and re-create it" (306). Wittman turns into an engineer with the intent to design a new apparatus for making epic drama.

I read Maxine Hong Kingston's *Tripmaster Monkey* as a meditation upon the relationship between art and social change. In light of the conflicted and heterogeneous formation called Asian America, Wittman Ah Sing advocates moving beyond its originary sixties meaning, which requires a great deal of imagination. Throughout the text, Wittman appears singly motivated by his desire to punch his way out of boxes that inscribe his identity as a Chinese American male. From an ideological standpoint, he is reacting against what Frank Chin has coined "racist love," otherwise known as liberal multiculturalism. Gayatri Spivak stated that multiculturalism as such is about "sucking difference out of difference."[20] The marginalized other, the powerless, the disenfranchised has become all too knowable. We recognize them easily; they fit into neat, predictable sociological categories. Wittman wants to normalize the Chinese so as to restore individual integrity and dignity to persons of Chinese ancestry.

For Maxine Hong Kingston, the ways the minority group and the dominant society "look" at each other lie at the heart of this novel. Chinese or Asian American culture is forged out of this dialectics of mutual gazing, and that the "ethnic" artist/writer might enlighten the process of looking by what Patricia Lin describes as "re-presenting representation."[21] In so doing, Kingston does not invoke the existence of the real Chinese versus the fake, nor does she rely upon the distinctions between the East and the West. Rather, by taking the readers/audience inside the mind of an "indigenous" deconstructionist/artist, she makes plain the process by which racial stereotypes are made and hence suggests how they can be unmade. To this end, there is nothing that can be said to be distinctively Chinese or not Chinese.

On another level, if we consider the time frame of the novel, set in the late sixties to early seventies, *Tripmaster Monkey: His Fake Book*[22] in its sardonic and humorous reimagining of Asian America, can be read as a critique of sixties identity politics from a postsixties, feminist standpoint. Unlike the cultural nationalists in the sixties, with their overtly masculinist approach, Wittman Ah Sing is essentially a pacifist, a poet at heart. Rather than promote a singular identity as Chinese American or Asian American, he advocates radically opening up possibilities of negotiating one's identity. An iconoclast to the end, he refuses to be appropriated either by the mainstream or by the ethnic left. Creating discomfort and shock is his preferred method of instigating social change.

The Return of the Real[23]

For Frank Chin, Chinese American or Asian American culture begins to take shape precisely when the artist/writer cuts loose from the gaze of white America. While some would disagree that one could ever be free from the gaze of others in the first place, Chin contends that obsession with white norms and values still acts as a formidable impediment against the making of a uniquely Asian American culture. In his introductory essay to *The Big Aiiieeeee!* (1991), Chin writes, "What if all the whites were to vanish from the American hemisphere, right now? No more whites to push us around, or to be afraid of, or to try to impress, or to prove ourselves to. What do we Asian Americans, Chinese Americans, Japanese Americans . . . have to hold us together? . . . For no matter how white we dress, speak, and behave, we will never be white."[24] Chin goes on to argue that cultural texts that are too mindful of the dominant white gaze inevitably yield "fake" Chinese American culture, which might draw popularity among the whites but that undermines the growth of a culture and identity, independently and uniquely Chinese or Asian American. He insists upon the existence of the "real" Chinese American culture that lay hitherto buried by the long legacy of Western imperialism. The return of the real comes in the form of ancestral Chinese gods and warriors inscribed in Confucian legends and folktales said to contain the unique values, morals, and thinking of the Chinese people. Chin remembers growing up in Chinatown and being exposed to the fairy tales and the heroic tradition at home and in public places. They were found in "figurines, statues, and calendar art" as well as in "toys, on flash cards, and in comic and coloring books." Moreover, he points out, they are even written into the by-laws of the tongs and associations.[25]

Chin's invocation of the "fake" and the "real" is rooted in his belief that life is war. A convert to the political philosophy laid out in Sun Tzu's *Art of War*, Chin declares, "Every human is born a soldier. All behavior is tactics and strategy."[26] He argues that "deception" lies at the heart of all warfare. Hence, one's survival depends upon being able to tell the difference between the fake and the real (xv). Translated into cultural politics, Chin believes, the viability of Chinese America depends upon defending the real Chinese America, rooted in "the Asian fairy tale and the Confucian heroic tradition," rather than the fake Chinese America whose description can be traced to sources in "Christian dogma and in Western philosophy, history, and literature" (xv). In short, China and Chinese America portrayed in the fake tradition are "the products of white racist imagination" (xi).

Chin is sharply critical of the integrationists and their version of Chinese America. He believes that the integrationist writers are consumed with the desire to become fully accepted by Anglo-America. Such a mentality requires internalizing the master narrative, which denigrates the culture and history of China and Chinese America. By giving up their "inferior" Chinese heritage and thereby adopting Western culture, Chin explains, they are made to think that they will be accepted by the dominant Anglo-America. Chin argues that such thinking arises from blind faith and belief in the goodness of white people, and he contends that their writing can only speak about a China and Chinese America rooted in a narrative that denigrates Chinese America and, consequently, engenders self-contempt.

Chin proposes an alternative: the construction of Chinese American culture based entirely on Chinese sources. Chin wants to fill in the missing content of Chinese American culture with sources that are uniquely Chinese or Asian. In the mid-seventies, he stated, in an essay entitled "Where I'm Coming from," "If we don't satisfy our need for Asian American myth, we'll continue as Asian Americans to draw upon the only myth that binds us all together now—the myth of white supremacy and yellow dependency."[27]

Even as I am critical of Chin's dogmatic and seemingly Luddite insistence upon the fake and the real, still I find his argument compelling, given the tendency of the West to delegitimize and orientalize the history and the traditions of the nonWest. Chin's retelling of Chinese American culture, even if positivistic, is a powerful testimony against the cultural practices of white racism. As the author himself argues, when the English settlers left England, they continued to study "the Magna Carta and Shakespeare"; so why should the Chinese give up their legends and fairy tales? Chin states that it was notably harder to preserve his own ancestral heritage: "We had to gather the stuff of the real the hard way. We had to ask, inspect, corroborate, challenge, and prove the factual, textual reality of the stuff and its place in Asian universal knowledge."[28]

In his novel, *Donald Duk* (1991), Chin explores how the protagonist's "identity crisis" is largely rooted in his ignorance of his ancestral heritage. The beginning lines of the novel describes the protagonist as a "model-minority" type who, being ashamed of his Chinese heritage and looks, desires to become white, a Chinese Fred Astaire. In a mocking tone, the narrator of the novel introduces the protagonist: "Would you believe anyone named Donald Duk dances like Fred Astaire? Donald Duk does not like his name. He is not a duck. He is not a cartoon character. He does not go home to sleep in Disneyland every night. The kids that laugh at him are very smart. Everyone at his private school is smart. Donald Duk is smart."[29] Donald's discomfort with his name signifies his being ill at ease with his Chineseness. Uncle Donald Duk (after whom he was named) believes that the American school is responsible for "pulling the guts out" of Donald and turning him "into some kind of engineer of hate for everything Chinese" (23). In school Donald listens to his teacher reading from a history text about China:

> The Chinese in America were made passive and nonassertive by centuries of Confucian thought and Zen mysticism. They were totally unprepared for the violently individualistic and democratic

Americans. From their first step on American soil to the middle of the 20th century, the timid, introverted Chinese have been helpless against the relentless victimization by aggressive, highly competitive Americans. (2)

The message comes loud and clear to Donald: The Chinese are "artsy, cutesy, and chickendick" (3). Understandably, then, the narrator tells us that Donald "does not like his name" and that he does not wish to invite any of his friends to his house, which, according to Donald, is "too Chinese" (10).

Indeed, his home stands a world apart from that of his school. Living in Chinatown, Donald cannot escape Chinese culture, particularly since his uncle and his father are incessantly inculcating him with Chinese tales. "You don't know the 108 heroes of the Water Margin, do you?" asks Uncle Donald, sounding indignant. Donald's father, on the other hand, dramatizes the Water Margin tales by building 108 airplanes. Every event and conversation between them contains a lesson about the Chinese heroic tradition. Unlike Robbie, the young boy in *Chickencoop Chinaman*, who, being surrounded by disillusioned, failed-father types, does not have a positive self-image, Donald can hardly avoid becoming Chinese, given the superb positive role models presented by his father and his uncle. Their intent is to impart a sense of the lost masculine, heroic identity to the American-born son, who is obviously ashamed of his emasculated Chinese identity.

The paragon of Chinese American male identity is found in Kwan Kung, whom Donald remembers as the man with a "red" face whom he saw "in pictures and statues all over Chinatown." Kwan Kung was a popular folk hero brought to America by Cantonese immigrants through the national epic, *The Romance of the Three Kingdoms*.[30] Legend has it that he "fought many battles, was brave, generous, loyal to the Han Dynasty . . . a powerful giant, nine feet tall . . . with a beard two feet long."[31] With a "swarthy" complexion and eyebrows which resembled the "phoenix," his whole appearance "inspired a feeling of terror," describes Chin. He wears both a scholar's robe and a general's uniform. Countering the post-1925 image of

Charlie Chan—the emasculated Asian male—stands the giant Kwan Kung, whose "masculinity" is never in question. And unlike the stereotype, Kwan Kung was characterized as one whose "strength of mind and body, individuality and loyalty, capacity for revenge, and essential aloneness are reminiscent of the rugged Western hero of American myth," stated Dorothy Rituko McDonald in her introduction to Chin's plays.[32] In the novel, Donald Duk comes to have a deeper understanding of Kwan Kung when his father has to play the part of the warrior god. In so doing, the father, emulating Kwan Kung, becomes the perfect role model for his American-born son. In *Donald Duk*, the search for the appropriate father figure throughout much of Chin's writings finally comes to rest.

In the end, the young protagonist comes around to affirming his Chinese identity. Finding his identity as a Chinese American man means realizing that he can do better than become a mere Chinese Fred Astaire. Through a series of dreams, Donald is able to make the vital connection that in fact there is a continuity from the heroic tales of China to the valiant life of his great-grandfather Lee, who settled in the Sierras, contrary to what he had learned in school.

With a new identity comes also a new strategy for survival in America. Echoing the author's belief that in the heroic tradition "life is war," Donald's father teaches his son how to live like a true warrior:

> History is war, not sport! You think if you are a real good boy for them [white America], do what they do, like what they like, get good grades in their schools, they will take care of you forever? . . . That is faith, sincere belief in the goodness of others and none of your own. That's mysticism. . . . So don't expect me to get mad or be surprised the bok-gwai never told our history in any of their books you happen to read in the library, looking for yourself. You gotta keep the history yourself or lose it forever, boy. That's the mandate of heaven." (123)

Having finally learned the meaning of "the mandate of heaven," Donald announces one morning that he does not wish to go to school, which is full of "stupid racists" (149). At the conclusion of the novel,

Donald has given up his dream of becoming the first Chinese Fred Astaire. Posing as a counternarrative to the Americanization thesis, *Donald Duk* is a story about one turning "Chinese." A crucial lesson Donald learns is that it is only as a Chinese that he can have proper relations with white America. And far from giving up on being Chinese, he can adopt some of the cultural forms of white America by simply "adding on" to his Chinese core rather than becoming absorbed by white America. His father introduces the rather liberating notion that the very act of adding on other cultures is in fact essentially Chinese:

> I think Donald Duk may be the very first American-born Chinese-American boy to believe you have to give up being Chinese to be an American. These new immigrants prove that. They were originally Cantonese, and did not want to be Chinese. When China conquered the south, these people went further south, into Vietnam, Laos, Cambodia, and Thailand. They learned French. Now they're learning English. They still speak their Cantonese, their Chinese, their Viet or Lao or Cambodian, and French. Instead of giving anything up, they add on. They're including American in every thing else they know. And that makes them stronger than any of the American-born, like me, who had folks who worked hard to know absolutely nothing about China, who believed that if all they knew was 100 percent American-made in the USA Yankee know howdy doodle dandy, people would not mistake them for Chinese." (42)

While Chin's construction of a Chinese American culture founded on purely Chinese texts entirely independent of white insertions/ disruptions/interpretations may prove to be empowering for a people who have been traditionally defined, objectified, and appropriated in the orientalist discourse, it is still lacking and inadequate in other respects. According to his separatist logic, the Chinese are not passive, deferring, reserved, or fatalistic but rather are irreverent, aggressive, valiant, and practical. The need to distinguish the "real" Chinese from the stereotype seems to necessitate black-and-white distinctions. Inherent in this line of thinking is the proclivity to over-simplify, idealize, and objectify the Chinese people.

Ben Tong, a Chinese American scholar of China and Chinese America, agrees that knowing one's roots can be "very empower-ing," but he criticizes Chin for "picking and choosing" only those elements that fit into his theory of a masculinist Chinese America. For instance, Chin fails to acknowledge the multifaceted nature of Confucianism, which not only engendered the heroic tradition of the folk but also gave rise to a repressive, highly patriarchal ideology that under the state apparatus left a long-lasting imprint on the psyche of people both in China and in Chinese America. Given his idealized rendition of China, Chin is forced to say that "patriarchy does not exist in China" and that it is merely "an invention of Westerners," contradicting the observations of many others.[33] "The imperial ver-sion of Confucianism was male-dominated to the bone," according to Ben Tong.[34] Even as Chin renounces the binary construction of the East versus the West in orientalist discourses about China, he is forced to defend from a culturally pure or absolutist stance that the East and the West do exist. To illustrate, he posits that the genre of autobiography is purely Western. Hence, any Chinese American who writes an autobiography is necessarily an assimilationist who, like St. Augustine, is really writing a book of "confessions" renouncing his/her pagan/Chinese-ness in order to gain acceptance into the Chris-tian/Western civilization. According to Chin, the cultural boundaries defining Chinese America are quite narrow. In the final analysis, Chin is in fact unable to free himself from the white gaze that engendered the orientalizing discourse of the East and the West in the first place.[35]

Chin's vision of Chinese America is exclusionary in other ways. As evidenced in the very gendered construction of his novel, *Donald Duk*, the female voice is inconsequential. The females in the novel are at best ornamental to the predominantly male-centered plot and often serve as negative models of what is deemed by the author to be proper Chinese American sensibility. Donald's mother and his two sisters are nothing more than gross caricatures of people consumed with assimilationist desire. Typically, it is Donald's mom who offers up comments such as "Does it really matter if it's real?" referring to

Chinese fairy tales (164). As an outsider to the father-son dialogue, she admits to not understanding her "pagan husband," who is always "persecuting Christians" (164). Like the women of his novel, the women of Chinese America appear to have no place, function, or existence for Chin except as reminders of the absence of a clear Chinese American identity. Since Chinese patriarchy is entirely a "Western invention," women's voice is not central to the articulation of Chinese American identity. What results is a construction of Chinese America antithetical to the Chinese American feminist need to deconstruct socially codified notions of the masculine and the feminine.

Frank Chin wants to be able to say that he is himself free of the white gaze. But this is an impossibility. Asian American culture emerges somewhere between the desire to be free of the gaze and the hope of creating something new outside it. All the writers mentioned thus far promote the view that it is more important to pay attention to the creation of a new language, tradition, and criteria for determining Asian America than to establish a permanent fixed identity and an impermeable tradition. At other times, Chin suggests—in spite of his insistence upon the return to the original and the real—that culture, even the very best of it, must change with the times. In *Donald Duk*, the carefully crafted Water Margin airplanes are not preserved, but go up in smoke on Chinese New Year's Eve.

Signifying the fluid and versatile nature of Chinese American identity, both Chin and Kingston are drawn to the symbol of the Chinese Monkey King. Survival rather than dogma or idealism lies at the root of Monkey's actions. Wittman is the modern-day reincarnation of Monkey King, the warriorlike mythological trickster figure from Wu Cheng-en's sixteenth-century novel *The Pilgrimage to the East*. Wittman is firmly anchored to Chinese culture, but he is also subject to change. For Chin the monkey becomes an apt symbol for "the migration theme in the Chinese story." Chin states that "like Monkey, wherever the Chinese go, there is a Chinaman," which is to say that "Monkey assimilates everything, but is not assimilated by anything."[36]

Even as he is punished by the gods for breaking taboos, Monkey manages to escape difficult situations through trickery. In one episode, Monkey goes on a long pilgrimage with a redeemed monk in order to retrieve Buddhist scriptures. The monk, being spiritual, devout, and unquestioning, refuses to engage in violence when he comes up against travelers disguised as devils. Unlike the monk, Monkey is able to see through their disguises, and he breaks the taboo of violence by attacking the thieves. If life is war, Monkey is a good soldier who can survive its snares and insults, through trickery, cunning, and disguises. Given the history of Asian America, it is no wonder that both Kingston and Chin find their hero in the Monkey King.[37]

Chinatown Revisited

Donald Duk revisits Chinatown and tells a tale for Chinese American sons to grow up on, and in that respect, the book comes to resemble Pardee Lowe's *Father and Glorious Descendant*. However much Chin may protest the analogy between his book and that of Lowe, both stories paint a positive picture of Chinatown. By showcasing his family as a representative success story of Chinese America, Lowe wanted to convince America that the modernist impulse could coexist with Chinese traditionalism at a time when China—which was said to have slept through the centuries—came under the judgment of those who waited to see if China was indeed capable of catching up with the West. For Chin, *Donald Duk* is his answer to "everyone who despised Chinatown," who wondered "how did the sucker survive?"[38] But in his eagerness to paint a positive picture, he is forced to become silent about issues of class in the same way that Lowe presented his own merchant class background as the norm. Thus the picture that emerges in Chin's novel is out of synch with the Chinatown that Peter Kwong described in his most recent book, *Forbidden Workers* (1997).[39] In *Donald Duk* there are no sweatshops. In Kwong's work, undocumented workers live precarious lives; they are understandably less consumed with questions concerning what stories their sons will grow up on than they are about when and how they will pay off their debt of passage. Chin's novel remains at best an allegorical, didactic novel about the importance of reclaiming

Chinese ancestral tales in order to survive in America. For a fifth-generation Chinese American male whose roots go deep into the early Chinese history in California, Chinatown still looms large as the mainstay of Chinese America. Its survival depends upon keeping the stories of the old-timers alive and passing them down to their sons. The progeny of post-1949 immigrants are less likely to identify with the Chinatown of Chin's imagination.

Beyond "Grandfather's Stories": Shawn Wong's *American Knees*

Shawn Wong takes up the challenge that Wittman poses to Asian Americans: to become a "part of the daily love life of the country, to be shown and loved continuously" until Asian Americans can no longer be rendered "inscrutable."[40] In his second novel, *American Knees* (1995), Wong has left the project of telling his "grandfather's" stories—the subject of his earlier novel, *Homebase*—for a soap-opera-esque love story between a Chinese American man in his forties and a young Amerasian or Eurasian woman whose ethnic identity is inextricably enmeshed with their love interests. In an age when racial boundaries are less clearly drawn, a middle-aged activist from the sixties comes to rethink what it means to be an Asian American.

That he falls in love with a Eurasian puts interracial unions central to the larger discussion of ethnic identity. Conventional thinking, which tended to emphasize the notion of a pure "race," discouraged interracial matings, as they were said to be diluting the "race," and those involved in the interracial coupling frequently were saddled with the label "race traitors." They were said to trade in their ethnicity in order to gain a higher social and economic status in white society through marriage. Raymond Ding at first has misgivings about his attraction to Aurora because she is partially white. He doesn't want to feel like a sellout. As a product of the sixties who has long internalized the call to repudiate white norms and values—including the idealization of white feminine beauty—Raymond finds himself in a difficult place. His feelings toward Aurora only heighten his anxiety about losing his Chineseness, which is based on a conceptualization of identity politics left over from the sixties. Eventually, Raymond comes to the realization that marrying out does not necessarily mean throwing away ethnicity or self-identity. Aurora teaches him to embrace a postethnic perspective of identity that underscores the artificial notion of pure races as social constructs, as well as to adopt the view that subjects occupy multiple positions as we's. One need not favor one affiliation over the others.

Before romance enters in, however, Raymond has to resolve a messy divorce. He is worried that his wife might get custody of his ethnicity. Betraying his own anxiety about his identity as a Chinese American male, Raymond, in the wake of his divorce, wonders if "someone could be a lapsed Chinese, in the same way people became lapsed Catholics."[41] Confirming his fears, his lawyer tells him, "You won't even be Chinese after your wife's attorney gets through with you" (1). Appropriately, the novel begins with Raymond, who had come of age in the late sixties, having to reassess his notion of what it means to be a Chinese American male in the 1990s. Unable to shed the essentializing ways in which his Chinese American identity has come to be defined, he is always straining to fit into a politically correct version of being an Asian male. In this story, the orphan from his first novel has reached middle age and finds himself less sure of his identity as a Chinese or Asian American. The story does not contain the usual antics about one searching for one's roots. Rather it is a novel about renegotiating an Asian American male identity in a society that has become more diverse and visibly culturally heterogeneous.

The novel follows the trajectory of one who moves beyond the identity politics of the sixties and eventually comes to embrace a more pluralistic and fluid notion of ethnic identity. Through his encounter with Aurora, he comes to reevaluate the meaning of being Asian American. When Raymond and Aurora meet for the first time, they cannot help but regard each other with suspicion and disdain. As people who have come to internalize the dominant representations of Asians in America, they see each other initially as caricatures. From a distance, Aurora tries to size Raymond up with any number of stereotypes of the Asian male outfit. That he doesn't wear a "Polo trademark" rules out Korean and that he doesn't come with a "cheap haircut with greasy bangs falling across the eyebrows, squarish goldrimmed glasses" discounts him as being Chinese (36). Similarly, Raymond cannot speak easily with Aurora, for he knows better than to utter aloud what he notices about how her eyes slant nicely in the light and about her mixed racial heritage, for she may consider his remarks lewd, orientalizing, or politically incorrect. Even as they eventually fall in love with one another, this palpable tension between them grows and causes them to break up temporarily.

The difficulty in their relationship arises from the fact that they cannot simply ignore the ways in which the dominant gaze has come to define the Asian male and female. They can't ever just be normal with each other: "Sometimes, Raymond, I just wanted you to say that I'm the center of your life and that you love me. Why does the whole world around that center always have to be something called Asian America?" (60–61) In many ways, the rift between Aurora and Raymond is symptomatic of the gender rift in Asian America, given how Asian women have been hyperfeminized and how the men have been made effeminate.[42] This defining gaze of the dominant society becomes a pervasive and invasive omnipresence in their relationship that even the very intimate act of lovemaking cannot always shut out. The story ends with their getting back together, however guardedly; this is testimony to their willingness to see and discover themselves anew. In a way, this novel, as the first Asian American love story, marks the mending of the gender rift oft noted in Chinese American writing since the seventies.

Aurora shows Raymond that one way to be purged of the racialized stereotypes of the Asian is to voice them and to attack them with humor. Early in his relationship with Aurora, Raymond realizes that political correctness is rooted in repressive politics that afford mere tolerance at the sacrifice of any real intimacy. The text is full of jokes about events and persons within Asian America. In fact, the book might be subtitled *The Complete Book of Asian American Stereotypes*. From the girl with "daikon legs" to the man who wears "baggybutt polyester pants," no one escapes the ridicule and the laughter. Laughing with people who have been similarly grouped into an ethnic camp about the very ways in which they have been named is liberating, as the heavy load of names stacked high is temporarily lifted.

The picture of Asian America depicted in the novel is refreshing and unorthodox. It features a cast of Asian Americans, none of whom fit a predictable mold. Jimmy Chan is the editor in chief of a news journal; Brenda and Betty, far from being submissive, have their own careers; and Aurora is an aspiring photographer. Nor are they simply ghettoized within Asian America. Sylvia Beacon-Yamaki, Raymond's lawyer, is a white woman married to a Japanese American, and Miles is the African American boyfriend of Julia, Aurora's younger sister. The very heterogeneity within Asian America challenges the stereotypical view of Asian Americans. At the same time, however, the picture Wong paints of the Asian American professional class is perhaps too optimistic. In light of increasing attacks against affirmative action and the infringement of other rights of people of color, Asian Americans in Wong's novel never seem to be in the least bit worried about their economic status or at all concerned about the glass ceiling effect that continues to ghettoize Asians in certain sectors.

Turning Chinese or Jewish?: Gish Jen's *Mona in the Promised Land*

In synch with the heterogenous vision of America promoted in *American Knees*, the novel *Mona in the Promised Land* (1996) by Gish Jen moves away from the notion that a Chinese American has but two choices, to turn Chinese or to assimilate into Anglo-America. Ethnicity for Mona is much like a costume she tries on for size. Nothing can be said in essence to be Chinese or Jewish or American. In the following scene, Mona and Sherman, her Japanese boyfriend, talk again a few years after their first meeting. They speak about their ethnic identity. "Are you American now?" Mona asks. "Have you switched?" He answers, "One hundred percent. Are you surprised?"

His answer prompts Mona to speak candidly about her own identity which is not WASP, and not black, and not as Jewish as Jewish can be, and not from Chinatown either.[43] Being "American," explains

Mona, "means being whatever you want" (49). For Asian Americans whose immigrant parents, embracing the American dream, moved their families into well-to-do suburbs like "Scarshill" America—a takeoff on Scarsdale, New York—the negotiation of their identity is riddled with unlikely forces peculiar to suburbia. Scarshill, for instance, is predominantly Jewish. Unlike the Chinese American students who in the sixties were as much influenced by the Oakland Black Panthers as they were by Mao Tse-dong in China, Mona and Callie, living within the liberal Jewish community, are more likely to be enamored with the countercultural movement than with the kind of activism embraced by San Francisco State and UC Berkeley students. Mona is less concerned about what courses her school offers than about whether a Chinese American can become Jewish. As part of a social clique with Barbara, Seth, and others—all of whom are Jewish—Mona herself becomes an honorary member of the synogogue. She's even "been named the official mascot of the Temple Youth Group" (32).

In this novel, the author brings to the fore the much talked about Jewish-Asian connection. Numerous scholars have pointed to the similarity between the histories of the two groups in America. Given their emphasis on high achievement and upward mobility, belief in education, and their reputation as "model minorities" in the eyes of Anglo-America, it is not surprising that the Jews and Asians in America find themselves living adjacent to one another in suburbs like Scarshill.

The story revolves around a teenager named Mona, her older sister, Callie, and Helen and Ralph, their parents, whom the reader has already met in the author's first novel, *Typical American*. Her decision to turn Jewish is as much rooted in her desire to create an identity in opposition to that of her parents (symptomatic of teenage rebellion) as it is in her being accepted into the dominant circle of her "hip" friends, who happen to be Jewish.

Mona, a product of the sixties, is also influenced by the countercultural thinking embodied in Seth, her Jewish boyfriend. A product of liberal thinking, she comes to question her parents' values and practices. Contrary to her parents, whose primary allegiance to their family and business render them politically conservative on matters of race and class, the Reform Jews she encounters take up more fashionably leftist stance on matters ranging from race and alternative lifestyles to religion. When her parents refuse to hire black workers, she says that they are being racists. She is also critical of their seemingly single-minded focus on making money.

She is also attracted to Judaism for its emphasis on preserving tradition. "Prescriptions and rituals, holidays and recipes, songs. The Jews have books, they have games, they have tchotchkes. They have catalogs. And soon, G-d willing, so will Mona" (36). In other words, unlike Asians, who are relatively invisible, Jews in America have a recognizable presence.

Furthermore, becoming Asian is less appealing to Mona, perhaps because she does not see herself fitting into the stereotype of the demure Asian American woman. Miss Feeble, one of her teachers, for instance, has to tell her to "give someone else a chance to talk" in class (27). Mona does not fit into the typical model-minority mold. Mona contemplates what it means to be Chinese. She tries to discern whether being Chinese is anything like being Jewish. When her friend Barbara Gugelstein, says that being Jewish means "not forgetting" that she's Jewish (32), Mona tries to imagine what it would be like to forget she's Chinese. "It is easy [to forget] because by her lonesome she in fact often does. Out in the world of other people, though, Mona has people like Miss Feeble to keep the subject shiny" (32).

In contrast, Callie, Mona's older sister, who is attending Harvard-Radcliffe, traverses a different path and wants to turn more Chinese. Her African American roommate, Naomi, who is herself interested in Chinese studies, influences Callie to become more ethnically conscious, so she switches out of her French class and takes up Mandarin instead. Also, much to her parents' chagrin, she befriends Japanese and Korean students. She dresses in Chinese peasant garb, unaware of the irony of someone in her privileged position mimicking the uniform of peasants. As with Mona, it is hard to take Callie's whimsical conversion too seriously.

Mona in the Promised Land, then, provides a subtle critique of the identity politics of the sixties, which laid out but two choices to the ethnic minority: assimilation or separation from WASP America. Gish Jen gives a revisionist reading of the sixties in which members of the second generation, emerging out of the suburbanized middle class, negotiate their identity much differently from those who grew up in Chinatown. She insinuates that the process is messier if also a bit less serious than it is made out to be.

Without the connection to the old-timers in Chinatown, second-generation Chinese like Callie and Mona are divorced from the memory of the early Chinese and their struggles in America. As the American-born progeny of immigrant parents who fled China to escape communism and who have situated their families in posh East Coast suburbs, they are neither consumed with assimilationist desire to join WASP America nor ready to wholeheartedly embrace being "Chinese" or "Asian American." In spite of all the drama behind Mona and Callie's becoming Jewish or Asian American, ethnicity takes a backseat to class interests. In the end, the wayward daughters are reconciled to their mother as differences are resolved. Having outgrown their rebellious adolescence, they have indeed become respectable adults who have done nothing—much to the relief of their parents—to jeopardize their class status. As Sau-ling Wong suggests, a position that trivializes ethnicity in this way is perhaps indicative of someone who is writing from a privileged class position.[44]

Rethinking the Sixties

Mona Chang, Raymond Ding, and Wittman Ah Sing, who are young adults in the sixties, are engaged in rethinking the identity politics of their time. While it is widely agreed that the earlier conceptualization of Asian or Chinese America can no longer contain the growing heterogeneity today, their creators, rather than abandon history and forget the past, are remembering it differently. Often the forgotten, the easily overlooked subjects are brought up in the rethinking of the sixties. For instance, Wittman reminds us that not all Chinese came to America to dig for gold but that some came to play, with treasure chests full of costumes, plays, and poems. Mona Chang suggests that class affiliation in some instances is stronger than ethnic or racial ties. And Raymond Ding shows us that even diehard activists from the sixties can come to embrace a more postethnic perspective on identity.

Parenting the Immigrant Generation: Fae Myenne Ng's *Bone* and David Wong Louie's *Pangs of Love*

In contrast to Jen's novel, Fae Myenne Ng's *Bone* (1993) revisits Chinatown, where Leila, the narrator and main protagonist, works out the challenge of striking a balance between living her own life and taking care of her immigrant parents. She is in many ways the woman warrior grown up who is confronted with a reversal of roles. She must parent her aging immigrant parents, who—given their socioeconomic status—are bound to live out the rest of their lives in Chinatown, a predicament that the second generation does not necessarily share. The circumstances surrounding the death of her middle sister, Ona, and her own marriage to Mason, prompt Leila to reflect upon her position in relation to her parents and to Chinatown. As the oldest, Leila feels responsible for taking care of Leon, her stepfather, and her mother. Though orphaned by her real father, Lyman Fu, she adopts a surrogate father and inherits a family whose members have become increasingly dependent on her. At times, Leila herself is aware of the irony of her playing the role of a parent to her stepfather. Catching herself yelling at Leon in public, she realizes how it must seem to others watching on: "I started thinking about what other people thought, what they saw: This Chinese girl yelling at her old man."[45] Leon tests her patience with his wanderings; her mother circumscribes her freedom by trying to tie her daughter down. Leila, consequently, tries to protect her mother by delaying her own marriage plans. She wants to prevent her mother from "refeeling the mistake" by being forced to face "the bitterness of her own marriages." That is, Leila "wanted to protect her [Mah] from remembering the bad" (12). It is with much difficulty that she is able to tell herself that she cannot be made to pay for her mother's past mistakes, and that she cannot feel guilty for simply "having a better life than Mah" (12).

Her realization that immigrant life is "hard" makes it particularly difficult for Leila to walk away from her needy parents. In spite of the hardships, the memories of her childhood, however impoverished and circumscribed by economic necessity, give her a strong sense of who she is and strengthen her determination to stay with her parents.

> "Bones," I repeated. This was a funny that got sad, and knowing it, I kept laughing. I was surprised how much memory there was in one word. . . . Dove birds, we called them. We fed them leftover rice in water, and as long as they stayed plump, they were our pets. . . . But then one day we'd come home from school to find them cooked. Mah said they were special, a nutritious treat. She filled our bowls high with little pigeon parts: legs, breasts, and wings. She let us take our dinners out to the front room to watch *I Love Lucy*. Mah opened up a brown bag for the bones (30).

Unlike her memory of Mah, who was always around and working too hard, her memory of Leon is punctuated by periods of his long absence. Leon, whom she describes as a "deformed man," is a tragic figure, an old-timer whose get-rich-quick schemes never amount to much. Though an extravagant man at heart, whose love of adventure takes him out to the sea, he feels unmanly because he cannot support his family with a steady income. He spends his days hanging out with the other "do-nothing" old men at Portsmouth Square or in Salvation Army stores collecting "junk" parts for his eclectic inventions. Mah has had to become the main breadwinner, working as a seamstress in Chinatown sweatshops and later opening up a children's clothing store. Financial and other difficulties, such as Mah's illicit affair with Tommie and Ona's suicide, force them to separate.

The harshness and the difficulty of immigrant lives is symbolized in the material conditions of Chinatown. Walking into a woman's apartment in Chinatown, Leila is reminded of how "everything is hard" in immigrant life: "I'm reminded that we've lived like that, too. The sewing machine next to the television, the rice bowls stacked on the table, the rolled up blankets pushed to one side of the sofa. Cardboard boxes every where, rearranged and used as tools or tables or homework desks. The money talk at dinner time . . . cluttered rooms, bare lives . . . Everything is hard" (17).

Ona killed herself, Leila surmises, in part because she did not know how to escape the difficult life in Chinatown. In a self-effacing manner, Ona lived her life solely occupied with concerns of her family, particularly Leon. "Ona had no skin," remarks Leila, referring to the way she so completely identified with him. "Every time he lost a job, she went into a depression with him. When he got high on some scheme, she was drunk on it, too" (172). Unlike her youngest half-sister, Nina, who left Chinatown altogether, Ona "didn't have an out" (173).

Leila decides that the only way she is going to live with the situation is to shuttle back and forth between Chinatown and her own place with her boyfriend in the Mission. Mason is her way out. Unlike Chin's earlier protagonists, who decide to make a clean break with Chinatown altogether, or his later invention, Donald Duk, who comes to embrace it in all its glory, Ng's Leila, with a great deal more compassion, embraces the immigrant generation without having to glamorize their lives in Chinatown. Like the woman warrior who dreams of saving her parents orphaned by the land developers who take away their laundry shop, Leila is the American-born daughter grown up to become parent to her immigrant family. Crucially, though, she provides herself with a way out when she needs to seek refuge.

She finds a home in the company of other similarly situated second-generation Chinese Americans like Mason and Zeke. The author describes these people as being robust and healthy as compared to previous generations. And perhaps most promising of all, they are seemingly defiant and unfazed by the white dominant gaze. Zeke, for instance, stops a comedian in the middle of his act to shout, "Cut the fucken' Chinese jokes" (46). Mason also is not affected by the white gaze: "Mason is born and raised in Chinatown. Sometimes he's proud and sometimes he's not. . . . Mason likes to ski and he goes to Tahoe as much as he can. He doesn't care if he's the only

Chinese guy on the expert runs. But there is one thing he does not do and that is gamble because it is 'too Chinesy'"(183). This generation of American-born Chinese in Ng's novel are less tormented by the gaze of white America. As American-born Chinese located within a Chinatown-based, working-class background, they have an ethnic identity more likely to be negotiated between the tensile pull and tug of their immigrant parents' needs and those of their own.

David Wong Louie's *Pangs of Love* (1991), a collection of short stories, echoes back some of the same themes already discussed in *Bone*. In the short story "Pangs of Love," the notion of the orphaned (in the sense of belonging neither wholly in mainstream America nor in the immigrant community) American-born parenting a similarly abandoned immigrant generation is revisited. As with so many of Louie's short stories, ethnicity is a covert rather than an overt mark of difference. Relationships rather than ethnicity become the main preoccupation of his protagonists. The story is narrated by a thirty-five-year-old American-born son, who, when Mandy Millstein leaves him for another man, finds himself playing the role of "his mother's new apartment mate."[46] Abandoned by Mandy, he becomes the caretaker of his immigrant widowed mother. In spite of the vast cultural and linguistic gulf between them, the protagonist is drawn to the childlike simplicity of his mother. His mother, in his eyes, is as "innocent as a child," since "her mind isn't cluttered with worries that extend beyond food and family." At times, he has "the urge" to wrap his arms around her and "protect her" (77). In his otherwise barren bachelor existence, he is strangely content in his role, having adopted a surrogate child in his mother.

While the protagonist in "Pangs of Love" is abandoned by white America, in the story "Displacement," a young female artist decides to leave the old white woman, symbolizing white America. Mrs. Chow, a painter, has worked for the ailing widow for many years, and many times she has talked about leaving her and finding another line of work less degrading: "Now as she talked about leaving the widow, it wasn't the chores or the old woman that she gave as the reason. . . . This time she said she had a project in mind, a great canvas of a yet undetermined subject. But that would come, once she was away from that house" (24). Her primary motive for leaving the job is not the chores, the verbal insults, or the constant suspicion placed on her, but the old widow's presence, which stifles her spirit and suppresses her creativity. I read this story as a meditation upon the artistic process that is contiguous with the process of negotiating one's identity. As some Chinese American writers have already noted, the ever-present gaze of dominant America has tended to delimit possibilities for being Asian American. Perhaps the author is suggesting that it is only when one is able to move away from the defining gaze that one can begin to create something new. The story leaves us with Mrs. Chow rinsing off the other woman's perfumes from her hands, and leaving her in order to look for a new site where she may begin her not yet defined project.

Conclusion

Community is not built once-and-for-all; people have to imagine, practice, and re-create it.

—Maxine Hong Kingston in *Tripmaster Monkey*

Looking Back

The empty canvas is an apt metaphor to conclude the study
of the American-born Chinese. The canvas yet to be filled holds great
promise for Asian Americans. Over the decades, they have begun
self-consciously to develop a language with which to discuss what it
means to be American of Chinese or Asian descent. As a part of that
language there exists, as if to testify to the existence of distinctive
Asian American culture, a rich repository of familiar themes, motifs,
and recurring intertextual references to the history of American-born
experience dating back more than half a century.

When Frank Chin, from the vantage point of the nineties, looked
back into the history of American-born Chinese, he proclaimed that
the so-called identity crisis among the young was really nothing more
than the manifestation of "white supremacist" thinking. He hark-
ened back to the great debate of the 1930s to explain his position:
"The young Chinese American *Christians* [italics mine] bought into
the stereotype . . . when they pondered the burning question, 'Does
my future lie in China or America?' They asked the same question
again and again, . . . without once confronting the white supremacist phoniness of the question."[1] According to Chin's worldview
of extremes, one was either a heroic Chinaman or a self-hating,

Christianized, sycophantic worshipper of white America, and there is no room for pondering the meaning behind who these American-born young really were, what they thought, and in what circumstances they found themselves.

Such ruthless blaming of American-born youths from bygone eras appears absurd and signifies a refusal to understand what it meant historically to be Chinese in America. To be "Chinese in background" was never merely an adjective used to describe their primary identity as Americans. The color of their skin and the slant of their eyes prevented them from blending in by simply changing their surname or by seeking anonymity in a new town. That mark of ethnic difference became for many an insurmountable barrier that they could not hope to fully overcome. To say that the American-born generations faced an identity crisis is to say that it was not always easy to see through the seductive rhetoric of the great American melting pot, as opposed to the reality of their treatment as secondary citizens in spite of their American-born status. What pained them particularly was that there was a profound contradiction between what they learned in school—mainly, that as natives to America, they had every right to the privileges and rights belonging to them as citizens—and the fact of their exclusion from mainstream social, economic, and political life. How does one make sense of the injustice behind holding a degree in engineering, pharmaceutical science, medicine, or architecture only to find oneself working alongside one's parents within the confines of Chinatown?

In the exclusionary years from the thirties to the early sixties, there were but two responses to racism: the separatist response, characterized by a rejection of white America, and the accommodationist one, characterized by seeking acceptance by white America. In the pre–World War II years, the majority of American-born generations voiced a separatist or a nationalist sentiment rooted in their belief that they had a "Chinaman's chance" of making it in America. For some, that meant going to their ancestral homeland, a war-torn China, to build their future and to rebuild a nation. A resurgence of separatism prevailed once again during the late sixties, when Chinese American youths, along with other Asian Americans, formed a pan-Asian movement to address systemic and institutional forms of racism. Yet they differed from their forebears of the thirties in that they were not advocating going to China. In reclaiming America, they sought to change and reform it so as to make America their own.

The World War II era and the beginning of the cold war in the fifties were characterized by a much more accommodationist stance. With the doors of opportunity opening for the Chinese in the war industries, the American-born generations stepped forward as expert translators and inventors of Chinese American identity and culture. Posing as the "bridge" between the East and the West, the American-born generations turned their bicultural state into an entrepreneurial asset, working as tour guides, entertainers, dress designers, interior decorators, writers, and commercial artists. In good times and bad, riding the turbulent waves of shifting pubic opinion regarding the image of the Chinese, American-born youth made strategic use of their "Chineseness" in order to promote the most enabling condition for their social and economic advancement. And crucially, contrary to the Americanization perspective that typically described the second-generation Chinese as assimilationist, the American-born generations were in fact not seeking to blend in as much as they were seeking opportunities to highlight their ethnicity and turn it into a desirable cultural commodity. Listening to the voices of the Forbidden City entertainers, I learned that they not only could deconstruct the gaze of their white audience but also could play the part expected of them in order to make a living. Jadin Wong learned to wear a Chinadoll haircut and a tight chingsom with a high slit, upon the advice of white show business producers, but she also stepped out as the first Asian, female comic, defying the advice of her agent, who thought that she should stick to dancing.[2] By flaunting the image of the exotic Chinese female, Wong secured a place for herself in an industry that has traditionally shut out Asian Americans. Her story and that of many others show that, far from being model assimilationists consumed with the desire to be white, the second generation became active agents in shaping Chinese America.

Looking Ahead

The current discussion of Asian American identity is to be distinguished from the identity politics of the seventies, a period when the "ethnic" self sought ways to authenticate the "true" self as apart from the stereotypical rendition of the ethnic other. In the current discourse about identity, it is conceived as a process, something never complete and always in formation. As a discourse predicated on the politics of difference, the conversation about identity in the eighties and the nineties tends to emphasize the characteristics and experiences that distinguish the ethnic from the dominant society, while, at the same time, making ethnicity one among many factors that shape identity.

The postethnic perspective of the last two decades points to an identification process that goes beyond the choice between separation and integration into mainstream America. Influenced by the theorization of postmodernist thinking, the transnationalization of capital, and the liberalization of immigration policies allowing for the making of a much more enriched if heterogeneous Asian America, many Chinese and Asian Americans no longer saw the necessity of negotiating their ethnic identity with mainstream America. In Gish Jen's, Fae Myenne Ng's, and Frank Chin's novels, WASP America drops out of the picture altogether. Increasingly, it is harder to say what lies at the "core" of American culture. For postethnics like Wittman Ah Sing, a label such as "Asian American" would most likely prove too confining, even as Helen and Ralph in Jen's novel found its meaning nebulous. The general consensus is that while the term "Asian American" still might serve a useful political function for Asian America, on the cultural front, it has become increasingly confining or even meaningless.

A lesson from the sixties that is still well worth keeping among other truths, however, is this: the distinctiveness of the experience of the American-born. Their uniqueness defies explanation by any of the existing sociological theory on generations or the Americanization thesis. Their lives reveal as much about America and its institutions as they do about how they were shaped by it. From their annals, we learn that the narrowness of a society that refused the entry of

Chinese Americans was met and challenged by the vast generosity of imagination on the part of American-born generations, which they used to cajole their way into positions of privilege and rank. I am inclined to believe that the American-born Chinese, like the Monkey King, were superb tricksters. Through shifts and vicissitudes of public opinion, they changed their guise from era to era, and in the process learned that identity, far from being something that could be preserved and placed apart, was something that was made and unmade, depending on circumstance. Throughout their journey, the name of the game was survival, and if they could steal a little fun in the process, it was that much better. Through laughter and tears, we remember.

Notes

Introduction

1. Jadin Wong, interview with the author in New York City, August 1996. She is also featured in Arthur Dong's documentary film *Forbidden City, U.S.A.* (Los Angeles: A Deep Focus Production, 1989).
2. I use "American-born" interchangeably with "second-generation" and "Chinese American," except when it is obvious from the context that I am using the term collectively to include the foreign-born faction of Chinese America. Because I do not subscribe to the generation theory put forth by Marcus Hansen and others, I use the term "second-generation" to refer to American-born Chinese regardless of second-, third-, or fourth-generational status.
3. The term "riverbanks of life" comes from Maxine Hong Kingston, *The Woman Warrior: Memoirs of a Girlhood Among Ghosts* (New York: Knopf Publishing, 1976), 6.
4. By 1940, 49,483, or 64 percent, of the total Chinese population resided in seventeen cities of one hundred thousand or more. The largest urban centers were San Francisco (17,782) and New York City (12,753). Los Angeles was the third with 4,736, followed by Oakland (3,201). By 1950, the trend toward urbanization was nearly complete, with 99 percent of Chinese Americans living in urban areas. Homer Loh, "Americans of Chinese Ancestry in Philadelphia" (Ph.D. diss., University of Pennsylvania, Philadelphia, 1944), 34.
5. The term "postethnic" comes from David A. Hollinger, *Postethnic America: Beyond Multiculturalism* (New York: Basic Books, 1995). Hollinger describes the postethnic perspective of the eighties and the nineties in the following manner: "A postethnic perspective denies neither history or biology—nor the need for affiliations—but it does deny that history and biology provide a set of clear orders for the affiliations we are to make. . . . [It] does not suppose that boundaries of the same order will work for everyone, nor that communities of the same scope and scale are right for all" (119).
6. Kevin Scott Wong also makes note of this omission in the introduction to *Claiming America: Constructing Chinese American Identities During the Exclusion Era*, ed. Kevin Scott Wong and Sucheng Chan (Philadelphia: Temple University Press, 1998). He writes that *Claiming America* is in part an answer to the omission of second-generation studies and quotes Sucheng Chan on the subject in *Entry Denied: Exclusion and the Chinese Community in America, 1882–1943*, ed. Sucheng Chan (Philadelphia: Temple University Press, 1991), x.

7. A version of the chapter on the American-born Chinese in the 1930s by the author appears in *Claiming America* as an essay entitled "'Go West . . . to China': Chinese American Identity in the 1930s."

8. On the critical genealogy of the term "marginal man," I am indebted to the work of Henry Yu, "Thinking about Orientals: Modernity, Social Science, and Asians in Twentieth-Century America" (Ph.D. diss., Princeton University, 1995). He explains that in 1938, Everett Stonequist, a student of Robert Park in Chicago, completed his dissertation entitled "The Marginal Man: A Study in the Subjective Aspects of Cultural Conflict." The germ of his thinking was derived from Park's thinking on the assimilation of ethnic Americans. Park even sent Stonequist to Hawaii to study how "marginal" and "second generation orientals" played important roles in "race relations" there. Yu states that Park was perhaps inspired to adopt the term "marginal man" from a study conducted by his student, E. B. Reuter, "The Mulatto in the United States: A Sociological and Psychological Study," (Ph.D. diss., University of Chicago, 1919).

9. Typifying the assimilationist perspective, scholars like Nathan Glazer have long maintained that over a period of time any people of non-European ancestral heritage would eventually shed their ethnicity. He states, "This [nation] was to be a union of states and a nation of free individuals, not a nation of politically defined ethnic groups." Glazer believed that the retention of ethnic heritage was diametrically opposed to the Americanization process; and that cultural pluralism could lead to political factionalism. See Nathan Glazer, "The Emergence of an American Ethnic Pattern," in *From Different Shores: Perspectives on Race and Ethnicity in America*, ed. Ronald Takaki, (New York: Oxford University Press, 1994), 12. In his most recent publication, *We Are All Multiculturalists Now* (1998), Glazer shows himself to be a reluctant convert to cultural pluralism but, philosophically, he abides by his convictions, formulated in the seventies.

10. See Rose Hum Lee, *The Chinese in the United States of America* (Hong Kong: Hong Kong University Press, 1960), 396–404.

11. Another weakness in the traditional generational studies is the way in which the first, second, and third generations are rigidly defined, with no regard for the sociohistorical location of the subjects. One such theory of ethnic generation suggested by Marcus Hansen states that the first or the immigrant generation tries to retain its traditional ways from the old country. The second generation, however, rejects the "old fashioned ways of their parents and see themselves as Americans." The third generation is characterized as revealing a "lively interest in the history, literature, and art of the land of their forefathers." See Marcus Lee Hansen, *The Immigrant in American History* (New York: Harper and Row Publishers, 1940), 93, 153. Karl Mannheim also confirms the thesis that the second generation is typically accommodationist. See Karl Mannheim, "The Problem of Generations," in *Essays on the Sociology of Knowledge* by Karl Mannheim, edited by Paul Keeskemeti (London: Routledge and Kegan, 1959), 276–320.

12. Revisionist scholars like John Blassingame (1972), Eugene Genovese (1974), Herbert Gutman (1976), Robert Raboteau (1978), and Robert Blauner (1972), among others, underscored ethnic retention among ethnic and racialized Americans rather than its loss. Along this line of thinking, writers Susan E. Keefe and Amado M. Padilla wrote *Chicano Ethnicity* (1977), and Mario Garcia

Mexican Americans (1989), both of which focus on American-born genera-tions of Mexican Americans.

13. Frank Chin, introduction to *Aiiieeeee! An Anthology of Asian-American Writers*, ed. Frank Chin et al. (Washington, D.C.: Howard University Press, 1974), ix.
14. Lee, *Chinese in the United States of America*, 39–42.
15. Ronald Takaki, *Strangers from a Different Shore: A History of Asian Americans* (Boston: Little, Brown, and Co., 1989), 254.
16. Sucheng Chan, "Race, Ethnic Culture, and Gender in the Construction of Identities among Second-Generation Chinese Americans, 1880s to 1930s," in *Claiming America*, 127–128.
17. Sucheng Chan, "The Exclusion of Chinese Women, 1870–1943," in *Entry Denied: Exclusion and the Chinese Community in America, 1882–1943*, ed. Sucheng Chan (Philadelphia: Temple University Press, 1991), 105.
18. Ibid., 106.
19. Takaki, *Strangers from a Different Shore*, 235.
20. Robert Dunn, "My Future Lies in America," *Chinese Digest*, 15 May 1936, 3.
21. Editorial, "The Year Ahead," *Chinese Press*, 28 December 1951, 4.
22. Ben Tong, interview with the author, San Francisco, 11 October 1989.

1 *"Go West . . . to China"*

1. Thomas Chinn, "A Historian's Reflection on Chinese-American Life in San Francisco, 1919–1991," interviews conducted by Ruth Teiser, Oral History Office, The Bancroft Library (Berkeley, California: Regents of the University of California, 1993), 54.
2. Ibid.
3. For a more in-depth discussion of the social isolation of American-born Chi-nese, see the introductory chapter in Hsien-ju Shih, "The Social and Voca-tional Adjustments of the Second Generation Chinese High School Students in San Francisco," (Ph.D. diss., University of California, Berkeley, 1937). Thomas Chinn was one of the chief editors for *Chinese Digest*, a major con-duit for American-born generations. The newspaper is an invaluable resource for researching this time period. It was established in 1934 and folded in 1940. It was the first truly Chinese American newspaper in the English language. This publication served as a crucial venue for young Chinese Americans to voice their concerns as second-generation Chinese Americans. The articles mirrored their responses to and reflections on a variety of issues and con-cerns such as the Japanese invasion of China, the economic depression, their exclusion from the mainstream job market, the preservation of Chinatown against foreign entrepreneurial and cultural encroachments, and their involve-ment in the Chinese section of the 1939 World's Fair. Contents included happenings in China, Chinese art and tradition, news about San Francisco Chinatown as well as other Chinese American communities, and, occasion-ally, cultural and social essays on Chinese American life. For further discus-sion on the subject, see Julie Shuk-yee Lam, "The *Chinese Digest*, 1935–1940," in Chinese Historical Society of America, *Chinese America: History and Perspectives, 1987* (San Francisco: Chinese Historical Society of America, 1987), 119–137.

4. University of California, Berkeley, *Student Registry, 1935–1936*, The Bancroft Library at the University of California, Berkeley.

5. Nate R. White, "Chinese in America," *Christian Science Monitor*, 1 February 1941, 4.

6. Shih, "Social and Vocational Adjustments," 72.

7. White, "Chinese in America," 4.

8. Shih, "Social and Vocational Adjustments," 59.

9. Ethyl Lum, "Chinese During the Depression," *Chinese Digest*, 22 November 1935, 10.

10. Ibid.

11. Rodney H. Chow, interviewed by Emma Louie on 24 January 1978 in Los Angeles as part of the Southern California Chinese American Oral History Project sponsored by the Asian American Studies Center, University of California, Los Angeles and Chinese Historical Society of Southern California. Vol. II, Interview number 27.

12. Lum, "China During the Depression," 10.

13. David Gan, "A Letter to the Gan Family," in an unpublished manuscript, "History of the Gan Family," ed. Helen Gan and John Aston (San Francisco, 1991).

14. *Chinese Digest*, 22 November 1935, 8.

15. William F. Wu, *The Yellow Peril: Chinese Americans in American Fiction, 1850–1940* (Hamden, Conn.: Archon Books, 1982), 165–175.

16. Sax Rohmer, *Fu-Manchu: Four Classic Novels* (1916; repr. Secaucus, N.J.: Citadel Press, 1983), 94.

17. Harold R. Isaacs, *Scratches on Our Minds: American Views of China and India* (1948; repr. New York: The John Day Company, 1957), 119.

18. Wu, *The Yellow Peril*, 178.

19. Ibid., 179.

20. Ibid.

21. California State Emergency Relief Institute, "A Report of the State Emergency Relief Institute of Governmental Studies Administration, 1935–1944," 18, The Bancroft Library at the University of California, Berkeley.

22. Louise Chin, "I'm an American," *The Record*, 17 January 1935, 20.

23. Ibid.

24. Isaacs, *Scratches on Our Minds*, 157.

25. Ibid., 156.

26. Robert Dunn, "In America Lies My Future," *Chinese Digest*, 15 May 1936, 3; Kaye Hong, "Go West to China," 22 May 1936, 3.

27. Stanford University students wrote in on two separate occasions. See Firecrackers, *Chinese Digest*, 22 May 1936, 3, 14; 3 July 1936, 5, 14.

28. Dunn, "In America Lies My Future," 3.

29. Ibid.

30. Firecrackers, *Chinese Digest*, 3 July 1936, 5, 14.

31. Kaye Hong, "Go West to China," *Chinese Digest*, 22 May 1936, 3.

32. James Low, interview, from Victor G. and Brett de Bary Nee, *Longtime Californ': A Documentary Study of an American Chinatown* (1973; repr. Stanford, Calif.: Stanford University Press, 1986), 169.

33. Thomas Chinn, *Bridging the Pacific: San Francisco Chinatown and Its People* (San Francisco: Chinese Historical Society of America, 1989), 93, 162.

34. Bernard P. Wong, *Chinatown: Economic Adaptation and Ethnic Identity of the Chinese* (New York: Holt, Rinehart, & Winston, 1982), 37, 38.
35. Ibid., p. 40; U.S. Department of Commerce, Bureau of the Census, Fifteenth Census of the United States, 1930: *Population: General Report on Occupations*, vol. 5, 95–97.
36. Ernest O. Hanser, "Chinaman's Chance," *Saturday Evening Post*, 213:23 (7 December 1940), 85.
37. Grace W. Wang, "A Speech on Second-Generation Chinese in U.S.A.," *Chinese Digest*, 7 August 1936, 6.
38. Ben Fee, interviewed by Ben Tong and Kathleen Chin on 26 March 1975 in San Francisco as part of the Combined Asian American Resources Oral History Project at The Bancroft Library at the University of California, Berkeley, BANC MSS # 80/31C. Grace Lee Boggs is another activist who embraced socialism but had little to no dealings with the Chinese American community per se in the 1930s and 1940s. Born and raised on the East Coast, she attended Barnard College as an undergraduate and received her Ph.D. in philosophy at Bryn Mawr College. She deserves mention as she was an influential interpreter and translator of Karl Marx's writings and since she has been an activist for black liberation in America. Interestingly, FBI files describe her as an "Afro-Chinese."
39. Far East, "Engineers Needed in China," *Chinese Digest*, 10 January 1936, 2.
40. Ibid.; editorial, "Chinese Abroad as Ambassadors," *Chinese Digest*, 21 August 1936, 8.
41. In a telephone interview conducted in October 1989, Ben Tong relayed to the author than an estimated 20 percent of American-born Chinese went to China during this period; he based his observation on his interviews with San Francisco Chinese Americans. See also Chinn, *Bridging the Pacific*, 134.
42. Lim P. Lee, "An Interview with Dr. Charles R. Shepherd upon his Return from China," *Chinese Digest*, February 1937, 11.
43. See U.S. Department of Commerce, Bureau of the Census, "Immigration Statistics," *Statistical Abstract of the United States 1909–1933.*
44. Grace Lee Boggs, *Living for Change: An Autobiography* (Minneapolis: University of Minneapolis Press, 1988), 1.
45. Chinese Students Club at UC Berkeley, "A Statement from the Far Eastern Relations Committee of the Chinese Students Club," vol. 1 (14 September 1936), 1, The Bancroft Library at the University of California, Berkeley.
46. Firecrackers, *Chinese Digest*, 19 June 1936, 14.
47. Firecrackers, *Chinese Digest*, 22 May 1936, 14.
48. Hong, "Go West to China," 3.
49. Ibid.
50. Firecrackers, *Chinese Digest*, 19 June 1936, 14.
51. "Chinese Girdle for Second Relief Campaign," *Chinese Digest*, December 1937, 14.
52. Ben Fee, interview by Ben Tong and Kathleen Chin.
53. James Low, interviewed in Nee and Nee, *Longtime Californ'*, 170.
54. Firecrackers, Letter to the Editors, *Chinese Digest*, 3 July 1936, 5, 14.
55. Rodney Chow, interview by Emma Louie.
56. *Statistical Abstract of the United States* for the years 1938 to 1944 published by the U.S. Department of Commerce, Bureau of the Census, shows a

steady increase in the numbers of immigrants from China. The gap between those immigrating and those departing began to close, an indication that either those who repatriated were coming back and/or a smaller number of American-born were departing for China.

Year	Admitted from China	Departed for China
1934	231	2,225
1936	297	1,663
1940	920	968
1941	1,003	816

57. Hanser, "Chinaman's Chance," 87.
58. Ibid.
59. Chinn, *Bridging the Pacific*, 160; Chinn, "A Historian's Reflection," 105.
60. Kaye Hong, interview with the author, San Francisco, February 1990.
61. Robert Dunn, interview with the author, San Francisco, February 1990.
62. Ibid.
63. Hong, "Go West to China," 3.
64. Dunn, "In America Lies My Future," 3.
65. Ibid., 14.
66. Hong, "Go West to China," 13.
67. Ibid.
68. "A Statement from the Far Eastern Relations Committee of the Chinese Students Club," 1.
69. Firecrackers, *Chinese Digest*, 3 July 1936, 5.
70. Book reviewed in *Chinese Digest*, 20 December 1935, 9.
71. Editorial, *Chinese Digest*, 13 November 1936, 13.
72. Ibid.
73. Ibid.
74. Ibid.
75. *The World Fair's Highlights* 1.7 (December–January 1937–38), 8; the Reverend Edwar Lee, interview with the author, September 1990.
76. Editorial, *Chinese Digest*, 10 April 1936, 8.
77. *The World Fair's Highlights*, 9, The Bancroft Library, University of California, Berkeley.
78. David Gan, interview with the author, San Francisco, January 1993.
79. *YMCA: Chinese Branch Historical Sketch*, 50th Anniversary, Chinese YMCA 1911–1961, The Bancroft Library; *The World Fair's Highlights*, 46.
80. *The World Fair's Highlights*, 19.
81. David Gan, interview with the author.
82. *The World Fair's Highlights, Clip Sheet*, no. 9, 1.
83. Judy Yung, *Unbound Feet: A Social History of Chinese Women in San Francisco* (Berkeley: University of California Press, 1995), 204.
84. Ibid.

2 *"Bridging the Gap"*

1. See Stuart Creighton Miller's *The Unwelcome Immigrants: Image of the Chinese, 1785–1882* (Berkeley, Calif.: University of California Press, 1969), 16–80. Miller establishes that American relations with China, by way of traders, diplomats, and missionaries, have influenced the American public's views of the Chinese starting as early as 1785. When the Chinese arrived on the

mainland in the mid-nineteenth century, these previously formed images of the Chinese prevailed.

2. In using the term "native informants" I am borrowing a concept from anthropology that refers to the practice of anthropologists' employing natives as field guides, translators, or tour guides, who provide the anthropologists with information about their cultural system. Given the imperialistic overtone associated with such a practice, the term "native informant" often has taken on a negative connotation. I use it here not to pass moral judgment upon the Chinese American native informants, but simply to point to their role/position vis-à-vis the dominant society.

3. Rodney H. Chow, interviewed by Emma Louie on 24 January 1978 in Los Angeles as part of the Southern California Chinese American Oral History Project, sponsored by the Asian American Studies Center, University of California, Los Angeles, and the Chinese Historical Society of Southern California. Vol. II, interview no. 27.

4. Madame Chiang Kai-shek, "Fighting for the Same Cause," *Vital Speeches of the Day*, vol. 9 (March 1943): 303.

5. Margaret K. Lee interviewed by Beverly Chan on 26 January 1980 and 29 April 1980 in Los Angeles as part of the Southern California Chinese American Oral History Project sponsored by the Asian American Studies Center, University of California, Los Angeles, and Chinese Historical Society of Southern California. Vol. IV, interview no. 85.

6. Ronald Takaki, *Strangers from a Different Shore: A History of Asian Americans* (Boston: Little, Brown, and Co., 1989), 374.

7. David Gan, interview with the author, San Francisco, January 1993.

8. Takaki, *Strangers from a Different Shore*, 399.

9. William Hoy, "Americans of Chinese Descent," in *Lake Tahoe Christian Conference Papers* 1941 (Asian-American Studies Libary, University of California, Berkeley), 34. It is hard to ascertain how many people joined the Chinese Christian Youth organization, but their influence in the English-speaking sector of the Chinese American community on the West Coast was significant. The *Conference Papers* ran from 1940 to 1949. Some members of the editorial board of the *Chinese Digest* belonged to the organization. Any noteworthy event associated with the conference was annually published in the *Chinese Digest*. The theology of the group was one largely influenced by the liberal logic of the social gospel movement.

10. Ibid.

11. Walter Kong, "How We Grill the Chinese," *Asia*, vol. 42 (September 1942): 520.

12. Ibid.

13. Ibid.

14. Sucheng Chan, *Asian Americans: An Interpretive History* (Boston: Twayne Publishers, 1991), 121.

15. Takaki, *Strangers from a Different Shore*, 378.

16. For more information about the history of Chinese interracial marriage see Betty Lee Sung, *Mountain of Gold* (New York: Macmillan Press, 1967), 253–260. See also Sucheng Chan, *Asian Americans*, 59–61.

17. Ruth Hall Whitefield, "Public Opinion and the Chinese Question in San Francisco, 1900–1947" (master's thesis, University of California, Berkeley, 1947), 99.

18. Rose Hum Lee, *The Chinese in the United States of America* (Hong Kong: Hong Kong University Press, 1960), 48.
19. William C. Smith, "Born American But—" *The Survey Graphic* vol. 56, no. 168 (1 May 1946): 106.
20. Willard Tim Chow, "The Re-emergence of the Inner City: The Pivot of Chinese Settlement in the East Bay Region of the San Francisco Bay Area" (Ph.D. diss., University of California, Berkeley, 1974), 152.
21. Whitefield, "Public Opinion and the Chinese Question," 99.
22. Bernard P. Wong, *Chinatown Economic Adaptation and Ethnic Identity of the Chinese* (New York: Holt, Rinehart, and Winston, 1982), 154.
23. Lee, *Chinese in the United States*, 271.
24. Chow, "Reemergence of the Inner City," 152.
25. Ruth Benedict, *Race: Science and Politics* (New York: Modern Age Books, 1940), 255.
26. Gunnar Myrdal, *The American Dilemma: The Negro Problem and Modern Democracy* (New York: Harper and Row Publishers, 1944), lxxi.
27. Gunnar Dahlberg, *Race, Reason, and Rubbish: An Examination of the Biological Credentials of the Nazi Creed*, trans. Lancelot Hogben (New York: Columbia University Press, 1943), 198.
28. Ashley Montagu, *Man's Most Dangerous Myth: The Fallacy of Race* (1942; repr. New York: The World Publishing Company, 1964), 26.
29. Ruth Wong, interviewed by Jue Louie in *The Combined Asian American Research Project* (CAARP), November 1976, # MSS 78/123C, The Bancroft Library, University of California, Berkeley.
30. Harold R. Isaacs, *Scratches on Our Minds: American Images of China and India* (1948; repr. New York: The John Day Company, 1957), 174.
31. Ibid., 173.
32. See "How To Tell the Japs from the Chinese," *Life* vol. 11 (22 December 1941): 81–82; "How to Tell Your Friends from the Japs," *Time*, vol. 38 (22 December 1941): 33–34.
33. "No Certain Way to Tell Japanese from Chinese," *Science News Letter*, vol. 40 (20 December 1941): 394.
34. Lin Yutang's book, *My Country, My People* (New York: John Day Publishing, 1935), did not address the presence of Chinese in America. His silence on the matter of racial prejudice has brought a great deal of criticism from Chinese Americans like Frank Chin in his Asian American literary anthology *Aiiieeeee! An Anthology of Asian-American Writers* (Washington, D.C.: Howard University Press, 1974).
35. Lin Yutang, "The Birth of a New China," *Asia*, vol. 39 (March 1939): 174.
36. Yutang, *My Country, My People*, 44.
37. Yutang, "The Birth of a New China," 174.
38. Rufus Suter, "China and Modern Science," *Scientific American*, vol. 158 (March 1938): 144–145.
39. Ibid.
40. Ibid.
41. Ibid.
42. Ibid.
43. Lester Walker, "The China Legend," *Harper's Magazine*, vol. 192 (March 1946): 241.
44. Ibid.

45. Amanda Boyden, "Changing Shanghai," *National Geographic*, vol. 72 (October 1937): 487.
46. Ibid., 488.
47. George Kin Leung, "Peiping's Happy New Year," *National Geographic*, vol. 70 (December 1936): 749.
48. Mildred Hand, "Mr. Chu—Modernist," *Asia*, vol. 36 (March 1936): 211.
49. See Renato Rosaldo, *Truth and Culture* (Boston: Beacon Press, 1989), 68–87.
50. James Burke, "Eunuchs of Peiping," *Life*, vol. 26 (21 February 1949): 17.
51. Ibid.
52. Dorothy Graham, "The Chinese Mind," *Catholic World*, vol. 164 (January 1947): 306.
53. Ibid.
54. Samuel G. Blythe, "Chinese Cooks," *Saturday Evening Post*, vol. 205 (29 April 1933): 10.
55. Ibid.
56. Pearl S. Buck, "The Most Unforgettable Character I've Ever Met," *Reader's Digest*, vol. 49 (October 1946): 70.
57. Thomas Handforth, "The Story of Mei Li," *The Horn Book Magazine*, vol. 15 (July 1939): 236.
58. Hoy, "Americans of Chinese Descent," 34.
59. Ibid.
60. Ibid.
61. Ibid.
62. Takaki, *Strangers from a Different Shore*, 213.
63. Pardee Lowe, *Father and Glorious Descendant* (Boston: Little, Brown and Co., 1943), 34.
64. Richard Polenberg, *One Nation Divisible: Class, Race, and Ethnicity in the United States Since 1938* (New York: Penguin Books, 1980), 19.
65. Pardee Lowe, "The Good Life in Chinatown: Further Adventures of a Chinese Husband and His American Wife Among His Own People," *Asia* (February 1937), 127.
66. Jade Snow Wong, interview with the author, San Francisco, 25 June 1996.
67. Jade Snow Wong, *Fifth Chinese Daughter* (Seattle: University of Washington Press, 1989), vii.
68. Lorraine Dong, "The Forbidden City Legacy and Its Chinese American Women," *Chinese America: History and Perspectives*, 1992 (Los Angeles: Chinese Historical Society of America), 126.
69. Charlie Low, in Dexter Waugh, "Forbidden City," *Image Magazine*, Sunday insert in *San Francisco Chronicle*, 29 October 1989, 22.
70. Jadin Wong, interview with the author, New York City, August 1996.
71. Mary Mammon, interviewed in Arthur Dong's documentary film *Forbidden City, U.S.A.* (Los Angeles: Deep Focus Productions, 1989).
72. Paul Wing, interview with the author, San Francisco, July 1992.
73. Jadin Wong, interviewed in *Forbidden City, U.S.A.*
74. Mary Mammon, interviewed in *Forbidden City, U.S.A.*
75. Ibid.
76. Tony Wing, interviewed in *Forbidden City, U.S.A.*
77. Jadin Wong, interview with the author.
78. Noel Toy, interviewed in *Forbidden City, U.S.A.*
79. Mary Mammon, interviewed in *Forbidden City, U.S.A.*

170   *Notes to Pages 68–77*

80. Jadin Wong, interview with the author.
81. Lorraine Dong, "The Forbidden City Legacy," 134.
82. Ibid.
83. Toy Yat Mar, interviewed in *Forbidden City, U.S.A.*

3   *"To Become Still Better Americans"*

1. Rose Hum Lee, "Your Job and You," *Chinese Press*, 11 August 1950, 4. The English-language newspaper *Chinese Press*, published in San Francisco, was widely circulated in California and in the rest of the nation. It began in 1940 and ran intermittently until it became regularized as a weekly in 1947. Its last issue was published on 1 February 1952. The *Press* crucially served as an important mouthpiece for second-generation Chinese Americans in the Cold War period.
2. David Caute, *The Great Fear* (New York: Simon and Schuster, 1978), 21.
3. Athan Theoharis, *Seeds of Repression* (Chicago: Quadrangle Books, 1971), 11.
4. A. T. Steele, *The American People and China* (New York: McGraw-Hill Book Company, 1966), 33.
5. Harold R. Isaacs, *Scratches on Our Minds: American Views of China and India* (1948; repr. New York: The John Day Company, 1957), 193–194.
6. Ibid., 215–229.
7. Ibid., 225.
8. "The Squeeze," *Time*, vol. 53, no. 22 (26 November 1951), 27: "Chinese Torture," *Newsweek*, vol. 38 (26 November 1951): 26.
9. Richard Polenberg, *One Nation Divisible: Class, Race, and Ethnicity in the United States Since 1938* (New York: Penguin Books, 1980), 116.
10. Caute, *The Great Fear*, 21.
11. Theoharis, *Seeds of Repression*, 11.
12. Ibid.
13. Stephen J. Whitfield, *The Culture of the Cold War* (Baltimore, Md.: Johns Hopkins University Press, 1991), 80.
14. Polenberg, *One Nation Divisible*, 116.
15. "Case of Togetherness: Illegal Immigration of the Chinese," *Time* (20 January 1958): 17. Other mainstream publications spoke about the "problem" of Chinese immigration. See "Case of the Chinese Officers," *Nation* (29 September 1951): 252ff.; "Chinese in Slavery," *Newsweek*, vol. 47 (25 March 1956): 30 passim.
16. "Fear of Chinese Delay Walter Resolution Passage," *Chinese Press*, 14 April 1950, 4.
17. Ronald Takaki, *Strangers from a Different Shore: A History of Asian Americans* (Boston: Little, Brown, and Co., 1989), 418.
18. Editorial, "Cathay, U.S.A.," *Chinese Press*, 22 June 1951, 4.
19. Ibid.
20. "The Year Ahead," *Chinese Press*, 28 December 1951, 4.
21. Dr. Francis L. K. Hsu is a China-born scholar, trained as an anthropologist in the United States, professor of anthropology at Northwestern University, whose works include *Under the Ancestors' Shadow: Chinese Culture and Personality* (1948), *American and Chinese: Two Ways of Life* (1953), and *The Challenge of the American Dream: The Chinese in the United States* (1971).

22. Francis L. K. Hsu, "The Chinese as an American Citizen," *Chinese Press*, 10 February 1950, 3.
23. Rose Hum Lee, *The Chinese in the United States of America* (Hong Kong: Hong Kong University Press, 1960), 425.
24. Editorial, "Cathay, U.S.A.," *Chinese Press*, 22 June 1951, 4.
25. Bob Lee, "Acculturation of Chinese Americans," *Chinese Press*, 5 October 1951, 4.
26. Isaacs, *Scratches on Our Minds*, 219.
27. Whitfield, *Culture of the Cold War*, 160.
28. "Chinese No Reds Says Shavey Lee," *Chinese Press*, 27 October 1950, 4.
29. "Will China Stay Red?" *Chinese Press*, 8 September 1950, 4.
30. Rose Hum Lee, *Chinese in the United States*, 113.
31. Ibid.
32. Lee's dissertation was published as a monograph under the same title by Arno Press in 1978. Butte, Montana, was a frontier mining town with a relatively large population of around 40,000 at its height, 10 percent of whom were Chinese. As was well documented by Henry Yu, who wrote "Thinking About Orientals: Modernity, Social Science, and Asians in Twentieth-Century America" (Ph.D. diss., Princeton University, 1995, Rose Hum Lee used interviews and personal materials from her own family and protected their identity by labeling her sources in the appendix as "private documents." See Yu, pages 225–239.
33. Rose Hum Lee, *The Chinese in the United States*, 2.
34. Ibid., 1.
35. Ibid.
36. Ibid., 117.
37. Ibid., 17.
38. Ibid.
39. "Sociologist Cites Chinese Progress in United States," *Chinese Press*, 15 July 1949, 2.
40. Richard Polenberg, *One Nation Divisible: Class, Race, and Ethnicity in the United States since 1938* (New York: Penguin Books, 1980), 127–129.
41. Rose Hum Lee, *Chinese in the United States*, 273.
42. Chinese American Folklore Collection: Sayings file, at the American Folklore Archives, University of California, Berkeley; Bernard P. Wong, *Chinatown: Economic Adaptation and Ethnic Identity of the Chinese* (New York: Holt, Rinehart, and Winston, 1982), 94–95.
43. Jin Goodwin, "Come out of Chinatown," *Chinese Press*, 18 April 1950, 6.
44. "How to Tell Baghdad from Cathay," *Chinese Press*, 9 March 1951, 4 , 5; see also Rose Hum Lee, "The Decline of Chinatown in the United States," *American Journal of Sociology*, vol. 54, no. 5: 422–432.
45. Rose Hum Lee, *Chinese in the United States*, 123.
46. Ibid., 124–126.
47. Ibid., 273.
48. *Lake Tahoe Christian Conference Papers, 1949*, 2 at the Asian American Studies Library at the University of California, Berkeley.
49. Rose Hum Lee, *Chinese in the United States*, 18.
50. David Riesman, Nathan Glazer, and Reuel Denney, *The Lonely Crowd: A Study of the Changing American Character* (New Haven: Yale University Press, 1950), 48–63.

51. C. Y. Lee, *The Flower Drum Song* (New York: Dell Book Publishing, 1961), 110.
52. "Chinese Graduates in U.S. Universities," *Chinese Press*, 7 July 1950, 2, 8.
53. Ibid.
54. *Student Registry, 1948–1949*, at The Bancroft Library, University of California, Berkeley.
55. "Record Number of Chinese Students," *Chinese Press*, 10 December 1948, 13.
56. Rose Hum Lee was referring to Beulah Ong Kwoh's "The Occupational Status of the American-born College Graduates" (unpublished master's thesis, University of California, 1941). Like Lee, Kwoh did graduate work in sociology at the University of Chicago. At one point, the two women roomed with each other. (Beulah Ong Kwoh, interviewed by Jean Wong as part of the Southern California Chinese American Oral History Project Vol. II, Interview no. 27, sponsored by the Asian American Studies Center, University of California, Los Angeles and Chinese Historical Society of Southern California.)
57. Rose Hum Lee, "Your Job and You," *Chinese Press*, 11 August 1950, 4.
58. William Lloyd Warner, Marchia Meeker, and Kenneth Ellis, *Social Class in America: A Manual of Procedure for the Measurement of Social Status* (Chicago: Science Research Associates, Inc., 1949), v.
59. Ibid.
60. "A Sociologist Looks at an American Community," *Life* (12 September 1949): 108–118.
61. "Where Are You Going?" *Chinese Press*, 28 April 1950, 7. Other articles problematizing the link between educational degrees and their effect on professional advancement appeared in the Press. See Faye Lee, "Can College Degrees Insure Happiness?" (30 December 1949); "Inter-college Students meet at Stockton," (27 January 1940); and "Education for What?" (13 January 1950). In all these pieces, even as the writers point to the difficulty of securing a position on par with the level of one's education, the conclusion drawn is that better opportunities can come only with higher degrees.
62. See "Future Meds Found Here," *Chinese Press*, 24 March 1950, 7.
63. "June '50 Grads Strive for Practical Careers," *Chinese Press*, 26 May 1950, 7.
64. See "Nine Chinese Win UC Scholarship," *Chinese Press* (16 June 1950), 4; "Oakland Girl Valedictorian" (16 June 1950), 1; and "Portland's Pride: Thora Lee" (30 July 1948), 2.
65. "No Chinese American Juvenile Delinquency," *America* (6 July 1955) 93: 402; "Our Amazing Chinese Kids," *Coronet* (December 1955) 39: 31–36; "Why No Chinese American Delinquents? Maybe It's Traditional Respect for Parents," *Saturday Evening Post* (30 April 1955) 227: 12; "Americans Without a Delinquency Problem," *Look* (29 April 1958) 22: 75–81; "Chinatown Offers Us a Lesson," *New York Times Magazine* (6 October 1957): 49ff.
66. Hsu, *Americans and Chinese*, 10.
67. "Why No Chinese American Delinquents," 12.
68. "Chinatown Offers Us a Lesson," 49.
69. Ibid., 56.
70. "The Open Forum: 'Punk' Fights Harm Community," *Chinese Press*, 5 May 1950, 8.
71. Ibid.
72. Ibid.

73. "We're Not Jive-Happy Unambitious Kids, We Want Jobs, Says Teen-Girl," *Chinese Press*, 31 March 1950, 2.
74. "75 % Discrimination State Survey Says," *Chinese Press*, 13 January 1950, 1–2.
75. "Transition of Foreign to Native Borns Bare Problems," *Chinese Press*, 17 February 1950, 3, is based on an interview of Rose Hum Lee.
76. Rose Hum Lee, *Chinese in the United States*, 122.
77. *USA: The Permanent Revolution* (New York: Fortune Inc., 1951), 18.
78. Ibid.
79. Ibid., x.
80. Rose Hum Lee, *Chinese in the United States*, 430.
81. "Sociologist Cites Chinese Press in United States," *Chinese Press*, 15 July 1949, 2.
82. Virginia Lee, *The House That Tai-ming Built* (New York: Macmillan, 1963), 45.
83. "Chinese Study Encouraged for Better Citizenship," *Chinese Press*, 29 July 1949, 3.
84. Rose Hum Lee, *Chinese in the United States*, 117.
85. Whitfield, *Culture of the Cold War*, 22.

4 *"Claiming America"*

1. Franklin Odo, Mary Uyematsu, Ken Hanada, Peggy Li, and Marie Chung, "The United States in Asia and Asians in America," in *Roots: An Asian American Reader*, ed. Amy Tachiki et al. (Los Angeles: The Regents of the University of California, 1971), 224.
2. The notion "claiming America" was first invoked by Maxine Hong Kingston in her novel *China Men* (New York: Ballantine Books, 1977), 165–201.
3. By 1970, Asian Americans, numbering fewer than one and a half million, constituted less than 1 percent of the total U.S. population. In the same year, Chinese Americans numbered 431,583, and of that total, the native-born population constituted 53 percent. See William Wei, *The Asian American Movement* (Philadelphia: Temple University Press, 1993), 4–11. According to *Statistical Profile of the Chinese in the United States, 1970 Census*, prepared by Betty Lee Sung (Washington D.C.: U.S. Department of Labor, 1970), the Chinese in California between the ages of 15 and 24 constituted 23 percent of the Chinese population. They were set at 170,374. In the same state, 75.6 percent of Chinese American males between the ages of 18 to 24 were enrolled in school, and 61.7 percent of the females were enrolled.
4. Amy Uyematsu, "The Emergence of Yellow Power in America,"in *Roots: An Asian American Reader*, 9.
5. Ibid.
6. Yuji Ichioka quoted in "Minority Leaders to Address Orientals," by John Chang, *Daily Californian*, 28 June 1968, 2.
7. Floyd Huen, interview with the author, San Francisco, 20 September 1991.
8. Yuji Ichioka in "Minority Leaders," 2.
9. Mr. Long's letter was first published in the *Daily Bruin*, which was the campus paper for the University of California at Los Angeles. The letter was reprinted in *Gidra*, June 1969, 2. R. Wu responded to it in *Gidra*, July 1969, 2.
10. Keith Osajima, "Asian Americans as the Model Minority: An Analysis of the

Popular Press Image in the 1960s and 1980s," in *Reflections on Shattered Windows*, ed. Gary Y. Okihiro, Shirley Hune, Arthur A. Hansen, and John M. Liu (Pullman, Washington: Washington State University Press, 1988), 165–174. Among numerous articles on Asian American success in the popular press were the following: "Success Story of One Minority in the U.S.," *U.S. News and World Report* (26 December 1966): 73–78; "Success Story, Japanese American Style," *New York Times Magazine* (9 January 1966): 20–21, 33, 36, 40–41, 43.

11. Uyematsu, "Emergence of Yellow Power in America," 11.

12. Ibid., 13.

13. Betty Lee Sung, *Chinese American Manpower and Employment* (New York: Department of Asian Studies, City College of New York, 1975), 110, 112.

14. Ibid., 94.

15. Ibid., 121, 124.

16. Uyematsu, "Emergence of Yellow Power in America," 8.

17. Jean Quon, interview with the author, San Francisco, 20 September 1991.

18. Alfred Wong, interview with the author, San Francisco, 10 October 1991.

19. Robert Blauner was the first to theorize on the notion of "the internal colony." See "Colonized and Immigrant Minorities," in Blauner, *Racial Oppression in America* (New York: Harper and Row, 1972).

20. Ampo Fusai, "Asian Studies Symposium on Vietnam," *AAPA Newspaper* vol. 2, issue 1 (November 1969): 3.

21. Laureen Chew, interview with the author, San Francisco, 20 October 1991.

22. Paul Wong, "The Emergence of the Asian American Movement," *Bridge*, vol. 2, no. 1 (1973): 32.

23. Fusai, "Asian Studies Symposium," 3.

24. Ibid.

25. Floyd Huen, interview with the author.

26. Ibid.

27. Ling-chi Wang, "Mellow Yellow Myth Exploded," *Daily Californian*, 15 January 1969, 13.

28. Laureen Chew, interview with the author, San Francisco, 10 July 1991.

29. Henry Weinstein, "TWLF Forum Explains Strike Objectives," *Daily Californian*, 24 January, 1969, 16.

30. For a more detailed study of the strikes in 1968–69 at San Francisco State College and UC Berkeley, see the article by Mike Murase, "Ethnic Studies and Higher Education for Asian Americans," in *Counterpoint: Perspectives on Asian America*, ed. Emma Gee et al. (Los Angeles: Breene Lithograph, 1976) and chapter 5 in William Wei's *The Asian American Movement* (Philadelphia: Temple University Press, 1993).

31. "TWLF: Strike Issue Is Self-Determination," *Daily Californian*, 22 January 1969, 9.

32. Rob Moreno and John Bergez, "Ethnic Studies Stress Student Control," *Daily Californian*, 1 October 1969, 8.

33. "Chinese Students Association Criticized," (letter to the editor) *Daily Californian*, 2 May 1968, 8.

34. Ronald Lee "Chinese Students Debate," *Daily Californian*, 15 May 1968, 12.

35. Ling-chi Wang, interview with the author, Berkeley, California, 10 October 1991.

36. Buck Wong, "Need for Awareness: An Essay on Chinatown, San Francisco," in *Roots: An Asian American Reader*, 265.
37. Roger Daniels, *Asian America: Chinese and Japanese in the United States Since 1850* (Seattle: University of Washington Press, 1988), 29.
38. Ben Tong, interview with the author, San Francisco, 11 October 1989.
39. Ibid. This poem was recited to the author in the interview.
40. Bill Moore, "The Facts about Life in Chinatown," *San Francisco Chronicle*, August 11, 1969, 187; "Goodbye and Hello," *New Yorker*, vol. 40 (February 29, 1964): 24.; Vincent McHugh, "San Francisco: Little China," *Holiday*, vol. 29, (April 1961): 100.
41. Laura Ho, "Pigs, Pickets, and Bananas," *Gidra* (May 1969): 2.
42. Gordon Lau, interview with the author, San Francisco, 19 September 1991.
43. Simi Lee, "Gordon Lau: 'Chinatown Is a Gilded Slum,'" *East/West* (11 March 1970): 10; "Tutors Sought for Chinatown," *Daily Californian*, 10 October 1968, 2.
44. See Bill Moore's series in the *San Francisco Chronicle* from August 11 to 14, 1969. See also Kenneth Lamott's piece on the Chinatown activists and agitators in "The Awakening of Chinatown," in *Sunday L.A. Times*, 4 January 1970, 7,9, 10, 12, 14, 15.
45. Jean Quon, interview with the author.
46. Manuel Valencia, "Lack of Funds: Third World Undaunted," *Daily Californian*, 4 February 1970, 4.
47. Ling-chi Wang, interview with the author.
48. "Candidate Lau Urges Chinatown Multi-center," *East/West* (30 July 1969): 1, 5.
49. Stanford M. Lyman, *Chinese Americans* (New York: Random House, 1974), 33–41.
50. For further information about the deterioration of the tongs and the informal political structure of Chinatowns, see Peter Kwong, "Tongs, Gangs, and the Godfather," in *The New Chinatown* (New York: Hill & Wang, 1987).
51. Lyman, *Chinese Americans*, 40.
52. Ken Wong, "Help the Poor," *East/West* (16 April 1969): 2.
53. Mark J. Jue, "Former S.F. State Students Discuss 1968 Strike and Its Meaning Now," *East/West* (2 November 1983): 7.
54. Ling-chi Wang, interview with the author.
55. Laureen Chew, interview with the author.
56. Gordan Lau, interview with the author.
57. Jean Quon, interview with the author.
58. Laureen Chew, interview with the author.
59. Jean Quon, interview with the author.
60. Miya Iwataki, "The Asian Women's Movement—A Retrospective," *East Wind*, vol 2, no. 1: 8.
61. Pam Lee, "Miss Chinatown Farce," *East/West* (15 April 1970): 2.
62. Nellie Wong, "When I Was Growing Up," in *This Bridge Called My Back: Writings by Radical Women of Color*, ed. Cherríe Morraga and Gloria Anzaldúa, (Watertown, Mass.: Persephone Press, 1981), 7.
63. Margaret Woo, "Woman, Man = Political Unity," *Asian Women* (Berkeley: University of California, 1972), 115.
64. Ibid.

65. Ibid.
66. Ron Tanaka, "I Hate My Wife," *Gidra* (September 1969): 3.
67. Iwataki, "Asian Women's Movements," 8.
68. See William Wei, "Speaking Out: the Asian American Alternative Press," in *The Asian American Movement*.
69. Frank Chin, introduction to *Aiiieeeeee!:An Anthology of Asian-American Writers*, ed. Frank Chin et al. (Washington D.C.: Howard University Press, 1974), vii.
70. Ibid., viii.
71. Ibid., x.
72. Ibid.
73. "Who's Afraid of Frank Chin? Or Is It Ching?" *Bridge: The Asian-American Magazine* vol. 2 No. 2 (December 1972): 30.
74. Ibid., 31.
75. Frank Chin, "Chinamen, Chinks, and the CACA," *East/West* (11 February 1970): 7.
76. Frank Chin, *The Year of the Dragon*, in *Two Plays by Frank Chin* (1974; repr. Seattle: University of Washington Press, 1981), 90, 92.
77. Frank Chin, "A Chinese Lady Dies," in his *The Chinaman Pacific & Frisco R.R. Co.* (Minneapolis: Coffee House Press, 1988), 122. The story was originally published in 1968.
78. Frank Chin, *Chickencoop Chinaman*, in *Two Plays by Frank Chin* (Seattle: University of Washington Press, 1981), 6–8. The play was originally produced in 1972.
79. Shawn Wong, *Homebase* (1979; repr. New York: Plume Books, 1991), 9.
80. Maxine Hong Kingston, *The Woman Warrior: Memoirs of a Girlhood Among Ghosts* (New York: Vintage Books, 1975), 56.

5 *"Punching Our Way Out"*

1. Gish Jen, *Mona in the Promised Land* (New York: Alfred A. Knopf, 1996), 301.
2. Ronald Takaki, *Strangers from a Different Shore: A History of Asians in America* (Boston: Little, Brown, and Co., 1989), 420.
3. U.S. Department of Commerce, *1990 Census of Population: Asians and Pacific Islanders in the United States*, U.S. Dept. of Commerce, (Washington D.C.: U.S. Government Printing Office, 1993), 6, 7.
4. Takaki, *Strangers from a Different Shore*, 419.
5. When the United States established formal ties with China in 1979, the People's Republic of China was given a separate annual quota of 20,000 in addition to the 20,000 allowed per year under the 1965 immigration act. Hong Kong was given an additional quota of 600 per year to raise the total to 40,600 per year. For more information see Peter Kwong, *The New Chinatown* (New York: Hill and Wang, 1987), 4–5.
6. For further information, see Paul Ong, Edna Bonacich, and Lucie Cheng, "The Political Economy of Capitalist Restructuring and the New Asian Immigration," in *The New Asian Immigration in Los Angeles and Global Restructuring*, ed. Paul Ong, Edna Bonacich, and Lucie Cheng (Philadelphia: Temple University Press, 1994), 24–31.

7. Susan Koshy, "The Fiction of Asian American Literature," *The Yale Journal of Criticism* vol. 9, no. 2 (1996): 336.
8. Michael Omi and Howard Winant, *Racial Formation in the United States: From the 1960s to the 1990s*, 2nd. ed. (New York: Routledge, 1994), 128–30.
9. Timothy P. Fong, *The First Suburban Chinatown: The Remaking of Monterey Park, California* (Philadelphia: Temple University Press, 1994), 159.
10. David A. Hollinger, *Postethnic America: Beyond Multiculturalism* (New York, Basic Books, 1995), 106.
11. Ibid., 118.
12. For an in-depth discussion on the debate between the impulse to embrace a more denationalized or diasporic identity on the cultural front versus the political necessity of keeping the pan-Asian identity alive, see Sau-ling C. Wong, "Denationization Reconsidered: Asian American Cultural Criticism at a Theoretical Crossroads," *Amerasia Journal* 21: 1 & 2 (1995): 1–27.
13. U.S. Census Bureau, "Census Bureau Facts for Features, Asian and Pacific Islander American Heritage North," 2. http:/www.census.gov/Press-Release.
14. U.S. Department of Commerce, Economics, and Statistics Administration, Bureau of the Census, *We the Americans: Asians* (Washington, D.C.: U.S. Government Printing Office, 1993), 4; U.S. Census Bureau, "Census Bureau Facts for Features, Asian and Pacific Islander American Heritage Month," 2. http://www.census.gov/Press-Release.
15. U.S. Department of Commerce, Economics, and Statistics Administration, Bureau of the Census, Statistical Brief, "The Nation's Asian and Pacific Islander Population—1994" (November 1995). Available from: Asian and Pacific Islander Population Dept., Claudette E. Bennett or Barbara Martin, (301) 457-2402 or Statistical Briefs Dept., Robert Bernstein or Barbara Hatchl (301) 457-3011.
16. Maxine Hong Kingston, *The Woman Warrior* (New York, Vintage Books, 1975), 6.
17. It is widely believed in the field that Wittman is largely modeled after Frank Chin himself.
18. Maxine Hong Kingston, *Tripmaster Monkey: His Fake Book* (New York: Alfred A. Knopf, 1989), 9.
19. The notion that the artist committed to social transformation must not merely feed the apparatus of cultural production but must also seek to transform the apparatus itself is a concept espoused by Walter Benjamin. See Walter Benjamin, "The Work of Art in the Age of Mechanical Reproduction," in *Illuminations: Walter Benjamin, Essays and Reflections*, ed. and with an introduction by Hannah Arendt (New York: Schocken Books, 1969), 217–251.
20. For a more extensive critique of multiculturalism see Gayatri C. Spivak, "Questions of Multi-culturalism: Conversation with Sneja Gunew," in *The Post-colonial Critic: Interviews, Strategies, Dialogues*, ed. Sarah Harasym (New York: Routledge, 1990), 59–66.
21. See Patricia Lin, "Clashing Constructs of Reality: Reading Maxine Hong Kingston's *Tripmaster Monkey: His Fake Book* as Indigenous Ethnography," in *Reading the Literatures of Asian America*, ed. Shirley Geok-lin Lim and Amy Ling (Philadelphia: Temple University Press, 1992), 337.
22. The author's reference in the subtitle to the "fake book" takes on a double

meaning. Drawing from musical jargon that refers to the written chords to standard songs, the fake book can be read as a score written for pioneering Asian American artists like Wittman Ah Sing. A second meaning has to do with the distinction between the "real and the fake" raised by Frank Chin and others, as described in the introduction to the Asian American literature anthology *The Big Aiiieeeee!: An Anthology of Chinese American and Japanese American Literature* (ed. Jeffrey Paul Chan et al. New York: Penguin Books, 1991). Knowing how her first book, *The Woman Warrior*, published under the label of nonfiction, was criticized for being fake by her detractors— as it distorts ancient Chinese folk tales, focuses on Chinese patriarchy, and is purportedly written for a white audience—Maxine Hong Kingston perhaps wants to make absolutely clear that *Tripmaster Monkey* is fake, as in "fiction."

23. The term "Return of the Real" is taken from the title of a book by Hal Foster, *Return of the Real: the Avant-Garde at the End of the Century* (Cambridge, Mass.: The MIT Press, 1996).

24. Frank Chin, introduction to *The Big Aiiieeeee!: An Anthology of Chinese American and Japanese American Literature*, ed. Jeffery Paul Chan et al. (New York, Penguin Books, 1991), 2.

25. Ibid., 3, 4.

26. Ibid., 15; For more information behind Chin's philosophy that "life is war," see, Sun Tzu, *The Art of War*, trans. and with an introduction by Samuel B. Griffith (New York: Oxford University Press, 1963).

27. Frank Chin, "Where I'm Coming from," *Bridge: An Asian American Perspective* (July 1976), 29.

28. Frank Chin, *The Big Aiiieeeee!*, xv.

29. Frank Chin, *Donald Duk* (Minneapolis, 1991), 1; Chin may have been inspired by Arthur Dong's documentary film *Forbidden City, U.S.A.* (Los Angeles: Deep Focus Production, 1989), which featured a dancer named Paul Wing, who stated that his childhood dream was to become a Chinese Fred Astaire.

30. Frank Chin, *Two Plays by Frank Chin* (Seattle: University of Washington Press, 1981), xxix.

31. Ibid., xxvi.

32. Ibid., xxviii.

33. Frank Chin, interview with the author, Los Angeles, September 1992.

34. Ben Tong, interview with the author, San Francisco, January 1992.

35. Frank Chin, *The Big Aiiieeeee!*, 11.

36. Frank Chin, interviewed in "West Meets East: A Conversation with Frank Chin," Robert Murray Davis in *Amerasia Journal* 24:1 (1998): 91.

37. See *The Real and the Fake Monkey*, adapted by Zhang Cheng from the classical Chinese novel *The Journey to the West* (by Wu Chengen of the Ming Dynasty) (Beijing: Zhaohua Publishing House, 1983).

38. Frank Chin, interviewed in "West Meets East," 88.

39. See Peter Kwong, *Forbidden Workers: Illegal Chinese Immigrants and American Labor* (New York: The New Press, 1997).

40. Kingston, *Tripmaster Monkey*, 310.

41. Shawn Wong, *American Knees* (New York: Simon and Schuster, 1995), 1.

42. As Sau-ling Wong explains, within the orientalizing Western discourse about the "ethnic" other, ethnicity becomes gendered so that typically the Asian

American male is effeminized and the Asian American female is hyper-feminized. See Sau-ling Wong's "Ethnicizing Gender: An Exploration of Sexuality as Sign in Chinese Immigrant Literature," in *Reading the Literatures of Asian America*, ed. Shirley Geok-lin Lim and Amy Ling (Philadelphia: Temple University Press, 1992), 111–129.

43. Jen, *Mona in the Promised Land*, 231.
44. Sau-ling C. Wong, public lecture delivered at Princeton University on March 24, 1998.
45. Fae Myenne Ng, *Bone* (New York: Hyperion, 1993), 56.
46. David Wong Louie, "Pangs of Love," in *Pangs of Love: Stories by David Wong Louie* (New York: Plume Books, 1992), 75.

Conclusion

1. Frank Chin, "Come All Ye Asian American Writers of the Real and the Fake," in *The Big Aiiieeeee!: An Anthology of Chinese American and Japanese American Literature*, ed. Jeffery Paul Chan et al. (New York: Penguin Books, 1991).
2. Jadin Wong, interview with the author, August 1996.

Bibliography

1990 Census of Population: Asians and Pacific Islanders in the United States.
U.S. Dept. of Commerce. Washington, D.C.: U.S. Government Printing Office, 1993.

"Americans Without a Delinquency Problem." *Look,* 29 April 1958, vol. 22: 75–81.

Asian American Political Alliance Magazine, vols. 1 and 2 (1969–1970).

Benedict, Ruth. *Race: Science and Politics.* New York: Modern Age Books, 1940.

Benjamin, Walter. "The Work of Art in the Age of Mechanical Reproduction." In *Illuminations: Walter Benjamin, Essays and Reflections,* edited and with an introduction by Hannah Arendt. New York: Schocken Books, 1969.

Blauner, Robert. *Racial Oppression in America.* New York: Harper and Row, 1972.

Blythe, Samuel G. "Chinese Cooks." *Saturday Evening Post,* 29 April 1933, vol. 205: 10.

Boggs, Grace Lee. *Living for Change: An Autobiography.* Minneapolis: University of Minneapolis Press, 1988.

Boyden, Amanda. "Changing Shanghai." *National Geographic,* October 1937, vol. 72: 487.

Buck, Pearl S. *The Good Earth.* New York: The John Day Company, 1931.

———. "The Most Unforgettable Character I've Met." *Reader's Digest,* October 1946, vol. 49: 70.

Bulosan, Carlos. *America Is in the Heart.* 1943. Reprint, Seattle: University of Washington Press, 1973.

Burke, James. "Eunuchs of Peiping." *Life,* 21 February 1949, vol. 26: 17.

Carmichael, Stokeley, and Charles V. Hamilton. *Black Power: The Politics of Liberation in America.* New York: Knopf, 1967.

"Case of the Chinese Officers." *Nation,* 29 September 1951: 252ff.

"Case of Togetherness: Illegal Immigration of the Chinese." *Time,* 20 January 1958: 17.

Caute, David. *The Great Fear.* New York: Simon and Schuster, 1978.

Chan, Jeffery Paul, Frank Chin, Lawson Fusao Inada, and Shawn Wong, eds. *The Big Aiiieeee!: An Anthology of Chinese American and Japanese American Literature.* New York: Penguin Books, 1991.

Chan, Sou. "What America Means to Me." *American Magazine,* July 1949: 17.

Chan, Sucheng. *Asian Americans: An Interpretive History.* Boston: Twayne Publishers, 1991.

———., ed. *Entry Denied: Exclusion and the Chinese Community in America, 1882–1943.* Philadelphia: Temple University Press, 1991.

Chew, Laureen, interview with the author, San Francisco, 10 July 1991 and 20 October 1991.
Chiang Kai-shek, Madame. "Fighting for the Same Cause." *Vital Speeches of the Day.* March 1943, vol. 9: 303.
Chin, Frank. *The Chinaman Pacific & Frisco R.R. Co.* Minneapolis: Coffee House Press, 1988.
———. *Donald Duk.* Minneapolis: Coffee House Press, 1991.
———. Interview with the author, Los Angeles, September 1992.
———. *Two Plays by Frank Chin.* Seattle: University of Washington Press, 1981.
———. "Where I'm Coming From." *Bridge: An Asian American Perspective,* July 1976: 29.
Chin, Frank, Jeffery Paul Chan, Lawson Fusao Inada, and Shawn Hsu Wong, eds. *Aiiieeeee! An Anthology of Asian-American Writers.* Washington D.C.: Howard University Press, 1974.
Chin, Louise. "I'm an American." *The Record,* January 1935: 20.
"Chinatown Offers Us a Lesson." *New York Times Magazine,* October 6, 1957: 49ff.
Chinese Digest. A weekly English-language newspaper, San Francisco, 1934–1940.
Chinese Students Club. "A Statement from the Far Eastern Relations Committee of the Chinese Students Club." *Chinese Students Club Newsletter,* September 14, 1936, vol. 1: 1. The Bancroft Library, University of California, Berkeley.
Chinn, Thomas. *Bridging the Pacific: San Francisco Chinatown and Its People.* San Francisco: Chinese Historical Society of America, 1989.
———. "A Historian's Reflection on Chinese-American Life in San Francisco, 1919–1991." Interview by Ruth Teiser, Oral History Office, The Bancroft Library, University of California, Berkeley.
Chow, Rodney H. Interviewed by Emma Louie on 24 January 1978 in Los Angeles as part of the Southern California Chinese American Oral History Project sponsored by the Asian American Studies Center, University of California, Los Angeles and Chinese Historical Society of Southern California. Vol. II, interview no. 27.
Chow, Willard Tim. "The Re-emergence of the Inner City: The Pivot of Chinese Settlement in the East Bay Region of the San Francisco Bay Area." Ph.D. dissertation. University of California, Berkeley, 1974.
Clifford, James, and George E. Marcus, eds. *Writing Cultures: The Poetics and Politics of Ethnography.* Berkeley: University of California Press, 1986.
Dahlberg, Gunnar. *Race, Reason, and Rubbish: An Examination of the Biological Credentials of the Nazi Creed.* Translated by Lancelot Hogben. New York: Columbia University Press, 1943.
Daniels, Roger. *Asian America: Chinese and Japanese in the United States Since 1850.* Seattle: University of Washington Press, 1988.
Dong, Arthur. *Forbidden City, U.S.A.* Documentary film. Los Angeles: A Deep Focus Production, 1989.
Dong, Lorraine. "The Forbidden City Legacy and Its Chinese American Women." In *Chinese America: History and Perspectives.* Los Angeles: Chinese Historical Society of America, 1992.
Dunn, Robert. Interview with the author, San Francisco, February 1990.
East/West. English-language journal, San Francisco, 1969–1975.
East Wind. English-language journal, San Francisco, 1945–1948.

Fanon, Frantz. *The Wretched of the Earth.* New York: Grove Press, Inc., 1963.

Fee, Ben. Interviewed by Ben Tong and Kathleen Chin on 26 March 1975 in San Francisco as part of the Combined Asian American Resources Oral History Project at The Bancroft Library, University of California, Berkeley. BANC MSS # 80/31C.

Fong, Timothy P. *The First Suburban Chinatown: The Remaking of Monterey Park, California.* Philadelphia: Temple University Press, 1994.

Gan, David. "A Letter to the Gan Family." Unpublished manuscript, "History of the Gan Family," edited by Helen Gan and John Aston. San Francisco, 1991.

————. Interview with the author, San Francisco, January 1993.

Garcia, Mario. *Mexican Americans: Leadership, Ideology, and Identity, 1930–1960.* New Haven, Conn.: Yale University Press, 1989.

Gibbon, John Murray. *Steel of Empire: The Romantic History of the Canadian Pacific, the Northwest Passage of Today.* Indianapolis and New York: The Bobbs-Merrill Company, 1935.

Glazer, Nathan. "The Emergence of an American Ethnic Pattern." In *From Different Shores: Perspectives on Race and Ethnicity in America,* edited by Ronald Takaki. New York: Oxford University Press, 1994.

————. *We Are All Multiculturalists Now.* Cambridge, Mass.: Harvard University Press, 1997.

"Goodbye and Hello." *New Yorker,* February 29, 1964, vol. 40: 24.

Goodwin, Jin. "Come Out of Chinatown." *Chinese Press,* 18 April 1950: 6.

Gordon, Milton M. *Assimilation in American Life.* New York: Oxford University Press, 1964.

Graham, Dorothy. "The Chinese Mind." *Catholic World,* January 1947, vol. 164: 306.

Hand, Mildred. "Mr. Chu—Modernist." *Asia,* March 1936, vol. 36: 211.

Handforth, Thomas. "The Story of Mei Li." *The Horn Book Magazine,* July 1939, vol. 15: 236.

Hansen, Marcus Lee. *The Immigrant in American History.* New York: Harper and Row Publishers, 1940.

Hanser, Ernest O. "Chinaman's Chance." *Saturday Evening Post,* 7 December 1940, vol. 213, no. 23: 85.

Hollinger, David A. *Postethnic America: Beyond Multiculturalism.* New York: Basic Books, 1995.

Hong, Kaye. Interview with the author, San Francisco, February 1990.

"How to Tell the Japs from the Chinese." *Life,* 22 December 1941, vol. 11: 81–82.

"How to Tell Your Friends from the Japs." *Time,* 22 December 1941, vol. 38: 33–34.

Hoy, William. "Chinatown a Colorful and New World Community." *Chinese Press,* 18 April 1950, 6.

Hsu, Francis L. K. *Americans and Chinese: Two Ways of Life.* New York: Henry Schuman, 1953.

————. "The Chinese as an American Citizen." *Chinese Press,* 10 February 1950, 3.

Huen, Floyd. Interview with the author, San Francisco, 20 September 1991.

"Immigration Statistics." *Statistical Abstract of the United States, 1909–1933.* U.S. Department of Commerce, Bureau of the Census.

Isaacs, Harold R. *Scratches on Our Minds: American Views of China and India.* 1948. Reprint, New York: The John Day Company, 1957.

Iwataki, Miya. "The Asian Women's Movement—a Retrospective." *EastWind,* vol. 2, no. 1: 8.

Jen, Gish. *Mona in the Promised Land.* New York: Alfred A. Knopf, 1996.

———. *Typical American.* Boston: Houghton Mifflin, 1991.

Keefe, Susan E., and Amado M. Padilla. *Chicano Ethnicity.* Albuquerque, New Mexico: University of New Mexico Press, 1987.

Kingston, Maxine Hong. *China Men.* New York: Ballantine Books, 1977.

———. *Tripmaster Monkey: His Fake Book.* New York: Alfred A. Knopf, 1987.

———. *The Woman Warrior: Memoirs of a Girlhood Among Ghosts.* New York: Vintage Books, 1975.

Kong, Walter. "How We Grill the Chinese." *Asia,* September 1942, vol. 42: 520.

Koshy, Susan. "The Fiction of Asian American Literature." *The Yale Journal of Criticism,* vol. 9, no. 2 (1996): 335–348.

Kwoh, Beulah Ong. "The Occupational Status of the American-born College Graduates." Unpublished master's thesis, University of California, 1941.

———. Interviewed by Jean Wong on 29 May 1979 and 14 August 1979 as part of the Southern California Chinese American Oral History Project. Vol. II, interview no. 27.

Kwong, Peter. *Forbidden Workers: Illegal Chinese Immigrants and American Labor.* New York: The New Press, 1997.

———. *The New Chinatown.* New York: Hill and Wang, 1987.

Lake Tahoe Christian Conference Papers (1941–1943). Asian American Studies Library, University of California, Berkeley.

Lam, Julie Shuk-yee. "The *Chinese Digest,* 1935–1940." In *Chinese America: History and Perspectives, 1987.* San Francisco: Chinese Historical Society of America, 1987.

Lau, Gordon. Interview with the author, San Francisco, 19 September 1991.

Lee, Bob. "Acculturation of Chinese Americans." Editorial in *Chinese Press,* October 5, 1951, 4.

Lee, C. Y. *The Flower Drum Song.* New York: Dell Book Publishing, 1961.

Lee, Margaret K. Interviewed by Beverly Chan on 26 January 1980 and 29 April 1980 in Los Angeles, as part of the Southern California Chinese American Oral History project sponsored by the Asian American Studies Center, University of California, Los Angeles and Chinese Historical Society of Southern California. Vol. IV, interview no. 85.

Lee, Pam. "Miss Chinatown Farce." *East/West,* 15 April 1970: 2–4.

Lee, Rose Hum. *The Chinese in the United States of America.* Hong Kong: Hong Kong University Press, 1960.

———. "The Decline of Chinatown in the United States." *American Journal of Sociology,* vol. 54, no. 5: 422–432.

———. *The Growth and Decline of Rocky Mountain Chinatowns.* New York: Arno Press, 1978.

———. "Your Job and You." *Chinese Press,* 11 August 1950: 4.

Lee, Virgina. *The House That Tai-ming Built.* New York: Macmillan, 1963.

Leung, George Kin. "Peiping's Happy New Year." *National Geographic,* December 1936, vol 70: 749.

Lin, Patricia. "Clashing Constructs of Reality: Reading Maxine Hong Kingston's *Trickmaster Monkey: His Fake Book* as Indigenous Ethnography." In *Reading the Literatures of Asian America,* edited by Shirley Geok-lin Lim and Amy Ling. Philadelphia: Temple University Press, 1992.

Lin Yutang. "The Birth of a New China." *Asia*, March 1939, vol. 39: 174.
————. *My Country, My People*. New York: John Day Publishing, 1935.
Louie, David Wong. *Pangs of Love: Stories by David Wong Louie*. New York: Plume Books, 1992.
Lowe, Pardee. *Father and Glorious Descendant*. Boston: Little, Brown, and Co., 1943.
————."The Good Life in Chinatown: Further Adventures of a Chinese Husband and His American Wife Among His Own People." *Asia*, February 1937: 127.
Lum, Ethyl. "Chinese During the Depression." *Chinese Digest*, 22 November 1935: 10.
Lyman, Stanford M. *Chinese Americans*. New York: Random House, 1974.
Mammon, Mary. Interviewed in Arthur Dong's *Forbidden City, U.S.A.*
Mannheim, Karl. "The Problem of Generations." In *Essays on the Sociology of Knowledge by Karl Mannheim*, edited by Paul Keeskemeti. London: Routledge and Kegan, 1959.
Mar, Toy Yat. Interviewed in Arthur Dong's *Forbidden City, U.S.A.*
McHugh, Vincent. "San Francisco: Little China." *Holiday*, April 1961, vol. 29: 100.
Miller, Stuart Creighton. *The Unwelcome Immigrants: Image of the Chinese, 1785–1882*. Berkeley, Calif.: University of California Press, 1969.
Montagu, Ashley. *Man's Most Dangerous Myth: The Fallacy of Race*. 1942. Reprint, New York: The World Publishing Company, 1964.
Moore, Bill. "The Facts About Life in Chinatown." *San Francisco Chronicle*, August 11, 1969: 187, 188.
Murase, Mike. "Ethnic Studies and Higher Education for Asian Americans." In *Counterpoint: Perspectives on Asian America*, edited by Emma Gee et al. Los Angeles: Breene Lithograph, 1976.
Myrdal, Gunnar. *The American Dilemma: The Negro Problem and Modern Democracy*. New York: Harper and Row Publishers, 1944.
Nee, Victor G., and Brett de Bary Nee. *Longtime Californ': A Documentary Study of an American Chinatown*. 1973. Reprint, Stanford, Calif.: Stanford University Press, 1986.
Ng, Fae Myenne. *Bone*. New York: Hyperion, 1993.
"No Certain Way to Tell Japanese from Chinese." *Science News Letter*, 20 December 1941, vol. 40: 394.
"No Chinese American Juvenile Delinquency." *America*, 6 July 1955, vol. 93: 402.
Odo, Franklin, Mary Uyematsu, Ken Hanada, Peggy Li, and Marie Chung. "The United States in Asia and Asians in America." In *Roots: An Asian American Reader* edited by Amy Tachiki et al. Los Angeles: The Regents of the University of California, 1971.
Omi, Michael, and Howard Winant. *Racial Formation in the United States: From the 1960s to the 1990s*. New York: Routledge, 1994.
Ong, Paul, Edna Bonacich, and Lucie Cheng, eds. *The New Asian Immigration in Los Angeles and Global Restructuring*. Philadelphia: Temple University Press, 1994.
Osajima, Keith. "Asian Americans as the Model Minority: An Analysis of the Popular Press Image in the 1960s and 1980s." In *Reflections on Shattered Windows*, edited by Gary Y. Okihiro, Shirley Hune, Arthur A. Hansen, and John M. Liu. Pullman, Washington: Washington State University Press, 1988.
"Our Amazing Chinese Kids." *Coronet*, December 1955, vol. 39: 31–36.

Park, Robert. *Introduction to the Science of Sociology.* Chicago: University of Chicago Press, 1921.

Polenberg, Richard. *One Nation Divisible: Class, Race, and Ethnicity in the United States since 1938.* New York: Penguin Books, 1980.

Population: General Report on Occupations. Prepared by the Bureau of the Census, Fifteenth Census of the United States, 1930. Vol. 5: 95–97.

Quon, Jean. Interview with the author, San Francisco, 20 September 1991.

Riesman, David, Nathan Glazer, and Reuel Denney. *The Lonely Crowd: A Study of the Changing American Character.* New Haven: Yale University Press, 1950.

Rohmer, Sax. *Fu-Manchu: Four Classic Novels.* 1916. Reprint, Secaucus, N.J.: Citadel Press, 1983.

Rosaldo, Renato. *Truth and Culture.* Boston: Beacon Press, 1989.

Said, Edward. *Orientalism.* New York: Pantheon Books, 1978.

Shih, Hsien-ju. "The Social and Vocational Adjustments of the Second Generation Chinese High School Students in San Francisco." Ph.D. diss., University of California, Berkeley, 1937.

Smith, William C. "Changing Personality Traits of Second Generation Orientals in America." *American Journal of Sociology,* May 1928, vol. 33: 6.

———. "Born American But—." *The Survey Graphic* vol. 56, no. 168 [1 May 1946]: 106.

Spivack, Gayatri C. "Questions of Multiculturalism: Conversation with Sneja Gunew." In *Post-colonial Critic: Interviews, Strategies, Dialogues,* edited by Sarah Harasym. New York: Routledge, 1990.

"The Squeeze." *Time,* 26 November 1951, vol. 53, no. 22: 27.

"State Emergency Relief Institute of Governmental Studies Administration, 1935–1944." The Bancroft Library at the University of California, Berkeley.

Steel, A.T. *The American People and China.* New York: McGraw-Hill Book Company. 1966.

Strong, Edward K. *The Second Generation Japanese Problem.* New York: Arno Press, 1970.

Student Registry, 1935–1936, 1948–1949. University of California, Berkeley. The Bancroft Library at University of California, Berkeley.

"Success Story, Japanese American Style." *New York Times Magazine,* 9 January 1966: 20–21, 33, 36, 40–41, 43.

"Success Story of One Minority in the U.S." *U.S. News and World Report,* 26 December 1966: 73–78.

Sun Tzu *The Art of War.* Translated and with an introduction by Samuel B. Griffith. New York: Oxford, 1963.

Sung, Betty Lee. *Chinese American Manpower and Employment.* New York: Department of Asian Studies, City College of New York, 1975. Available from the National Technical Information Service in Springfield, Virginia.

———. *Mountain of Gold.* New York: Macmillan Press, 1967.

Survey of Race Relations Collection, Box #22, Folder 20, Hoover Institution Archives, Stanford University.

Suter, Rufus. "China and Modern Science." *Scientific American,* March 1938, vol. 158: 144–145.

Tachiki, Amy, Eddie Wong, Franklin Odo, and Buck Wong, eds. *Roots: An Asian American Reader.* Los Angeles: The Regents of the University of California, 1976.

Takaki, Ronald. *Strangers from a Different Shore: A History of Asian Americans.* Boston: Little, Brown, and Co., 1989.

Tanaka, Ron. "I Hate My Wife." *Gidra*, September 1969: 3.

Theoharis, Athan. *Seeds of Repression.* Chicago: Quadrangle Books, 1971.

Tong, Ben. Interview with the author, San Francisco, October 1989 and January 1992.

Toy, Noel. Interviewed in Arthur Dong's *Forbidden City, U.S.A.*

USA: The Permanent Revolution. New York: Fortune Inc., 1951.

U.S. Census Bureau, "Census Bureau Facts for Features, Asian and Pacific Islander American Heritage Month." http:/www.census.gov/Press-Release.

U.S. Census Bureau, U. S. Department of Commerce, Economics, and Statistics Administration, "The Nation's Asian and Pacific Islander Population—1994." (November 1995). Available from: Asian and Pacific Islander Population Dept., Claudette E. Bennett or Barbara Martin (301) 457-2402 or Statistical Briefs Dept., Robert Bernstein or Barbara Hatchl (301) 457-3011.

U.S. Census Bureau, U.S. Department of Commerce, Economics, and Statistics Administration, *We the Americans: Asians.* Washington, D.C.: U.S. Government Printing Office, 1993.

U.S. Department of Commerce, Bureau of the Census. "Immigration Statistics." *Statistical Abstract of the United States 1909–1933.*

Uyematsu, Amy. "Why the Cry for Yellow Power." *Gidra*, October 1959: 9.

———. "The Emergence of Yellow Power in America." In *Roots: an Asian American Reader*, edited by Amy Tachiki et al. Los Angeles: The Regents of the University of California, 1971.

Walker, Lester, "The China Legend." *Harper's Magazine*, March 1946, vol. 192: 241.

Wang, Ling-chi. Interview with the author. Berkeley, California, September 1991 and 10 October 1991.

———. "Politics of Assimilation and Repression: History of the Chinese in the United States, 1940–1970." Unpublished manuscript, Asian American Studies Library, University of California, Berkeley.

Warner, W. Lloyd, Marchia Meeker, and Kenneth Eells, *Social Class in America: A Manual of Procedure for the Measurement of Social Status.* Chicago: Science Research Associates, 1949.

Wei, William. *The Asian American Movement.* Philadelphia: Temple University Press, 1993.

White, Nate R. "Chinese in America." *Christian Science Monitor*, 1 February 1941: 4.

Whitefield, Ruth Hall. "Public Opinion and the Chinese Question in San Francisco, 1900–1947." Master's thesis, University of California, Berkeley, 1947.

Whitfield, Stephen J. *The Culture of the Cold War.* Baltimore: Johns Hopkins University Press, 1991.

"Who's Afraid of Frank Chin? Or Is It Ching?" *Bridge: The Asian-American Magazine*, December 1972, vol. 2, no. 2: 30ff.

"Why No Chinese American Delinquents? Maybe It's Traditional Respect for Parents." *Saturday Evening Post*, 30 April 1955, vol. 227: 12.

Wing, Paul. Interview with the author, San Francisco, July 1992.

Wing, Tony. Interviewed in Arthur Dong's *Forbidden City, U.S.A.*

Wong, Alfred. Interview with the author, San Francisco, 10 October 1991.

Wong, Bernard P. *Chinatown: Economic Adaptation and Ethnic Identity of the Chinese.* New York: Holt, Rinehart, and Winston, 1982.

Wong, Buck. "Need for Awareness: An Essay on Chinatown, San Francisco." In *Roots: An Asian American Reader*, ed. Amy Tachiki et al. Los Angeles: The Regents of the University of California, 1971.

Wong, Jade Snow. *Fifth Chinese Daughter*. 1945. Reprint, Seattle: University of Washington Press, 1989.

————. Interview with the author, San Francisco, 25 June 1996.

————. *No Chinese Stranger*. New York: Harper and Row Publishers, 1979.

Wong, Jadin. Interviewed in Arthur Dong's *Forbidden City U.S.A.*

————. Interview with the author, New York City, August 1996.

Wong, Kevin Scott, and Sucheng Chan, eds. *Claiming America: Constructing Chinese American Identities During the Exclusion Era*. Philadelphia: Temple University Press, 1998.

Wong, Nellie. "When I Was Growing Up." In *This Bridge Called My Back, Writings by Radical Women of Color*, edited by Cherríe Morraga and Gloria Anzaldúa. Watertown, Mass.: Persephone Press, 1981.

Wong, Ruth. Interview with Jue Louie in *The Combined Asian American Research Project* (CARP), November 1976. The Bancroft Library, University of California, Berkeley.

Wong, Sau-ling. "Ethnicizing Gender: An Exploration of Sexuality as Sign in Chinese Immigrant Literature." In *Reading the Literature of Asian America*, edited by Shirley Geok-lin Lim and Amy Ling. Philadelphia: Temple University Press, 1992.

Wong, Shawn. *American Knees*. New York: Simon and Schuster, 1995.

————. *Homebase*. 1979. Reprinted in New York: Plume Books, 1991.

The World Fair's Highlights. December–January 1937–1938, vol. 1, no. 7: 8. The Bancroft Library, University of California, Berkeley.

Wu, Cheng-en. *The Pilgrimage to the East*. New York: French and European Publications, Inc., 1991.

Wu, William F. *The Yellow Peril: Chinese Americans in American Fiction, 1850–1940*. Hamden, Conn.: Archon Books, 1982.

YMCA: Chinese Branch Historical Sketch, 50th Anniversary, Chinese YMCA 1911–1961, The Bancroft Library, University of California, Berkeley.

Yu, Henry. "Thinking about Orientals: Modernity, Social Science, and Asians in Twentieth-Century America." Ph.D. dissertation, Princeton University, 1995.

Yung, Judy. *Unbound Feet: A Social History of Chinese Women in San Francisco*. Berkeley: University of California Press, 1995.

Index

accommodationism, 156, 162n.11.
See also assimilationism;
integrationist logic

African Americans, 3; segregation
of Chinese Americans likened to
that of, 16

Afro-American Student Union, UC
Berkeley, 105. See also Black
Power movement

Aiiieeeee! An Anthology of Asian
American Writers (ed. Chin et
al.), 6, 115

Amerasia Journal, 115

American-born Chinese, see
Chinese Americans

"American-Chinese," 44, 79

American Dilemma, The (Myrdal),
47

American Heritage Foundation
convention of 1951, 74

American Knees (Wong), 11, 142–
145

Americans and the Chinese: Two
Ways of Life (Hsu), 89–90

anthropology, physical: Chinese
American children exploited for,
20; distinguishing Chinese from
Japanese, 50–51

anti-Chinese movement, 2–3, 8

anti-war movement, 1960s, 10, 98

art, and negotiation of identity, 153;
social transformation through,
132–133, 177n. 19

Art of War, the (Sun Tzu), xii, 134

Asian America: An Interpretive

History (Chan), 3

Asian-American community, as
coalition, 97–98, 158. See also
Yellow Power movement
demographics of, 98–101, 125–
126, 173n. 3; diversity of, and
"postethnic" perspective, 122–
130; literary culture of, 115–122;
violence against, 128

Asian American Political Alliance
(AAPA), UC Berkeley, 98, 99,
102, 105, 106, 112

Asian Community Center, 109

assimilation, of surrounding
culture, 140; by surrounding
culture, 79, 80–84

assimilationism, 4–6, 39, 148, 157,
162n. 9; and repressive politics
of cold war, 96; 1960s critique of,
99–100

Augustine of Hippo, Saint, 139

autobiography, postulated as purely
Western, 139

"avenue kids," 82. See also
suburbanization

"bananas," 82

Benedict, Ruth, 47

Benjamin, Walter, 177n. 19

biculturalism, 63

Big Aiiieeeee!, The (ed. Chan et al.),
133

Biggers, Earl Derr, 19

Bing Dai, Huey, 75

Black Panther Party, 101, 112

About the Author

Gloria Heyung Chun is currently teaching Asian American History at Bard College. She has an undergraduate degree from Cornell University and a Ph.D. in Ethnic Studies from the University of California at Berkeley. Her research interests include biographies of Chinese American women and race relations in urban centers.